CONCUSSION AND MILD BRAIN INJURY

NOT JUST ANOTHER HEADLINE

A COLLECTION OF EXPERIENCES
OFFERING HOPE, HELP AND HEALING

EDITORS

BONNIE NISH, MA
NICOLE NOZICK
CHELSEA COMEAU
PHYLLIS BASSETT

ISBN 978-1-931117-48-7

9 781931 117487 >

Item: CAMBI

Published by Lash & Associates Publishing/Training Inc.
100 Boardwalk Drive, Suite 150, Youngsville, NC 27596
Tel: (919) 556-0300

This book is part of a series on brain injury among children, adolescents, adults and veterans.
For a free catalog, contact Lash & Associates
Tel: (919) 556-0300 or visit our website *www.lapublishing.com*

LASH & ASSOCIATES PUBLISHING/TRAINING INC.

100 BOARDWALK DRIVE, SUITE 150, YOUNGSVILLE, NC 27596
TEL: (919) 556-0300 FAX: (919) 556-0900

WWW.LAPUBLISHING.COM

TABLE OF CONTENTS

FOREWORD

Vera Kinach

As a Speech-Language Pathologist with 30+ years of experience working with a variety of communication difficulties, there is one group of clients who seem to be greatly misunderstood, under-diagnosed and under treated. This group of people are those who have sustained a concussion or mild traumatic brain injury.

For the majority of these clients, many of them have no visible sign that they have sustained any type of injury, and yet even a mild to moderate blow to the head can wreak havoc in terms of communication, employment, relationships and life in general.

Most of my clients were told or simply thought that a few days off work would resolve any symptoms following their concussion. Many of them have attempted a return to work too soon. Most of them, unfortunately, found out the hard way that the easing of symptoms or recovery could range from weeks to months, and for some, even years.

Those who sustained their concussion due to a work-related or motor vehicle accident, may have had the benefit of receiving treatment through a concussion clinic or private therapy. Others may not have had any rehabilitation assistance at all.

Concussions have gained more publicity lately with major sports stories such as those found in hockey, football or soccer. However, little is said about the rehabilitation journey and what these celebrities have endured during their course of recovery. Of course, we all know about Mohammed Ali, but that is an extreme case of multiple severe blows to the head over a lifetime and does not reflect the common person who hurts their head. There is little out there in terms of general knowledge of what happens to regular folks, living their usual lives, who suffer an insult to the brain.

All people who suffer a concussion just want to get back to their normal lives. Yet, because they have no visible symptoms of "illness", they often are poorly understood by their family, friends, employers, and even physicians. So the pressure is on to get back to work and get back to normal living. Believe me, that is the one desire that all people with concussions long for. No one likes being away from their jobs or regular activities under these circumstances.

While most people with concussions appear "normal" on the outside and speak well at a basic conversational level, many common communication problems can occur:

Difficulty with:

- finding words
- processing verbal information, especially if presented quickly
- processing information in noisy environments or with multiple speakers
- retaining what is heard
- formulating and communicating thoughts
- staying on topic or keeping a train of thought
- focusing and attending to the conversation
- retaining what has been read
- maintaining focus/attention for reading
- composing written messages, difficulty spelling
- verbal fluency or stuttering
- excessive "brain" fatigue after concentrated attention and focus

Added to these problems, come the usual other symptoms which accompany concussion, such as fatigue, headache, pain, etc. These symptoms usually correlate directly with a decline in the ability to communicate efficiently. Subsequently, many people prefer the quiet of their own home where they can control their environment. This can become very isolating and lonely over the long term.

The people I have met through my work have been my greatest teachers in sharing with me their stories, frustrations, and goals. All of them just want to get their life back the way it was. Nothing more. Yet, many of them continue to suffer from anxiety with regards to performing adequately on the job, communication skills and appearing "cognitively okay".

In my experience, it seems that what people with concussion lack is information and support about what they have experienced. In a talk I presented to a group of clients about communication disorders and concussion, one person made a comment that spoke loud and clear to me. After I explained what types of communication problems one might expect following concussion, she raised her hand and commented that until she heard this information, she feared she was developing Alzheimer's disease. When she received the information about concussion and possible communication symptoms, she was encouraged that perhaps she could get better, instead of fearing a decline in cognitive functioning.

While there are many support groups out there for stroke, brain injury and other medical problems, there seems to be a lack of resources (outside of concussion clinics) for support of those who have experienced concussion. When this anthology of stories about concussion survivors was proposed, it seemed like a good opportunity to educate the public about concussions occurring in the lives of ordinary people.

If you or your loved one have experienced a concussion, speak to your doctor, find a concussion clinic and search for information about concussion. It is my hope that one day perhaps there can be a formal community group for those to support each other during the tumultuous period of recovery following concussion.

An Introduction

Bonnie Nish

Maybe my need to collect other people's stories was simply a desire to try to understand my own situation. To feel not so alone in what had become a life I had not chosen but that had been suddenly thrust upon me. Maybe it was a clear sightedness on my part in a moment of awareness that this was actually bigger than me and that it was something that needed to be addressed publicly. An unseen wound needing to be exposed and aired. Or maybe it was just one of "those impulses" brought on by a severe bong to the head.

A few months later, I started to have the idea of compiling people's stories into a book. It started as a thought, something that seemed to help but that originally I wasn't sure I would pursue. I had my own life to get back to after all, my own book of poetry to finish editing, my job, my PhD coursework to complete, my therapy practice to try to open. Then came a second hit to the head and what seemed just an impulse or a desire to understand what was happening to me and to stop feeling so alone, suddenly became a necessity.

It became a driving force, not only for my own healing, but for those countless others who were experiencing everything I was going through or more…

- For their families who struggled to understand what was happening to loved ones.

- For their friends who were trying to hang on through thick and thin but were thinning themselves in what they could do or bear.

- For the employers who kept jobs waiting or didn't.

- For the doctors who struggled to find ways to kindly tell their patients, yes they had changed and their grief was absolutely a part of finding themselves again.

- For the general public who hear so much about athletes who get hit in the head four, five, six times and are appalled, but don't understand why the woman on the bus is wearing sunglasses on a rainy day, or is covering her ears in a quiet restaurant.

We all need to know what happens when someone has a traumatic brain injury. Why? Because it can happen in a flash to someone we love. They may be walking down the street or they may be standing perfectly still and something hits them in the head causing the brain to shake, rattle and roll into this new existence. It could happen to you when one moment you are running to catch the bus to work in your crazy busy schedule and the next you are lying in a dark room totally unable to function in any way that seems to resemble anything you have ever known.

This book has been a wake up call for me in some ways. It is something more than I ever imagined. As I listened and read people's stories I could see how individual they were, but I could also see the consistencies in their stories. In the symptoms they spoke of that lingered years later. I was told I would heal at the end of the weekend after I was first hit.When I didn't, I was told it would likely take me three to six months to heal. When this didn't happen, no one seemed to be able to say how long. When I was hit in the head a second time all my symptoms that were beginning to heal came back. Almost two years after the initial injury I no longer know when some of my symptoms will disappear. I do know that I am a different person than I was before the injury. Not too many other people see it. It is funny when it is something like your brain. It is the part of your body that most defines who you are. We don't usually think of this. We just exist.

Today I can tell you as I write this and I get tired, it took all I could do to read all the submissions. Not because they were bad or good, they all had something to offer. Some just weren't the right fit. I struggled on some days to keep them with me, to remember their details. To know I had even read them. On others they were there like an old friend, so welcome. They were all important. They all affected me in some way. They were all read numerous times and considered. They all had something of significance to say.

I am not so alone after reading them all. I am in not such a hurry to reclaim my life after sitting with these brain stories. I can go a step at a time now to what lies ahead and discover a new me. I too grieved for what I had lost, big time. But sitting in with others' stories makes me realize how important community and connection are. I have always believed it. This book makes me live it to the fullest. While it isn't a community I wanted to be a part of or create, it is something that is necessary, even if we only touch one another for a brief moment. It is a way of understanding what not many others get. Our coming together and understanding is a way of helping others to cope, see and be with those who are suffering from mild brain injury or concussion.

I hope this book touches, aides, moves you. I am grateful for the time I have spent here with these stories. I am a different person because of them.

Working with the other editors on this was real a joy. I thank them for their input, patience and friendship.

Bonnie Nish

Second Hand Concussion

Ali Denno
Bonnie Nish's Daughter

I didn't realize how difficult every day would be after my mom's initial concussion. I assumed I would check on her throughout the night and soon enough our lives would keep going as usual. However, everything within our lives drastically changed overnight. Her speech started to go and it became a guessing game as to what she was trying so desperately to get out. She slept most of the day, became depressed, couldn't walk a straight line, couldn't drive, and couldn't eat. Her usual keep busy personality was gone for the time being and it was a strange light in which to see her. I didn't fully realize the amount I had taken on, until I started to have a build up of frustrations that I would take out on others instead of telling my mom I couldn't do all of this by myself. There is a huge shift when someone can't communicate properly and is struggling to gain some form of self back. It is hard to watch and especially hard knowing there isn't a huge amount you can do for them.

When you think of a concussion or at least for me, I never thought of such a thing as concussion syndrome. I now know just how real and life changing it can be. Within the first few months, it was as if I was living with the shell of a person. She became so withdrawn and all I could do was try my best to make life a little bit easier. I became the household's grocery shopper, cleaner, and overall form of comfort. I spent most of my time with my mom, trying to understand what I could do to help her step forward instead of back. I spent a lot of time telling her not to push herself, to lie down, to not see too many people. I soon felt like a nagging mother to my own mother.

I started to become more and more concerned as her short term memory started getting worse when she began leaving her keys in the door, leaving her phone and car keys in the oddest places, and most concerning, leaving the oven on. These may sound like traits of someone without a concussion, but it was scary for me to spend the night elsewhere or be out knowing she might leave the oven on all night. It got to the point where every night before bed I would check the door to make sure her keys weren't there and check the oven to make sure it was off. I would even text her when I wasn't there just to make sure the oven was off.

People who weren't living in our household and saw her intermittently assumed she was progressing to the point that she was almost back to normal. This was by far one of the more frustrating parts of the past few years. I wanted my mom to not try to hide the fact that she wasn't fine, that people would talk to her instead of wait until she left the room to get to the truth of how she really was. I was angry at the fact that the people who cared the most for her couldn't ask her how she was doing to her face and I was constantly being told to take care of her. I was taking care of her, I knew every last detail of what made it too much for her to handle.

My life was changed along with my mom's, her life was of course changed more drastically than mine but I still felt the shift. I felt like I needed to always be there, not let her suffer through this alone, only it got to the point that I stopped going out with friends and made my boyfriend at the time suffer through with me. He and my friends took a lot of my frustrations when they didn't have to, and I am sure that it put a strain on those relationships.

When my mom got her second concussion, I laughed. There wasn't any other reaction to have. The fact that she was hit in the same place was incredibly funny and scary to me. She had already gone through so much and this was just a set back that made me so terrified that this time would be worse than the first one. The same symptoms came back, more and more problems with Workman's Comp came up, and frustrations rose in both of us. I started to get increasingly more outwardly frustrated with her, and frankly I came to resent her. My dad and doctor both confessed their concern for me, seeing that I was constantly angry and tense which they feared would soon eat away the positive parts of me. I then started being honest with my mom, mentioning things that she did that felt to me like guilt tripping and I know she didn't do all of this purposely. She became more and more aware of the fact that she was the mother and I was the daughter and for a while it did feel like it had shifted. I started to see her become more independent and rely on other people less. I felt ease in my life but still carried guilt in myself that I wasn't helping as much as I should be.

It wasn't until September of 2014 that we both felt a big shift in our reliance on one another. I went through a rough time in my own life, and she was there for me. I felt her step back as well, letting me gain parts of my own life back and figure out what I needed. I grew up rather quickly from nineteen to twenty-two; was working, going to school and had become a caretaker. I grew up because I didn't really have a choice; I wasn't going to go about my life knowing my mom needed the support every day to keep going and to keep healing. It has been almost three years since her first concussion. I have personally gone through many changes over these past three years and have seen my mom and I grow past any issues that arose. She is working full time, driving every day and gaining her old life back, little by little. I am finishing school, working and traveling. We both are silently aware of just how hard this time has been. We know just how appreciative we are of one another.

GIVE PAIN A VOICE

Luanne Armstrong

It was one of those casual encounters in the grocery store, a neighbour, not someone I know well. I had seen her husband earlier. He stood at the entrance to an aisle. His face was white, and his body thin. Community gossip was that his cancer is worse and I could see what that word, worse, meant in his face. I passed his wife, with an easy, "Hello, how are you" A standard greeting that means nothing. Or today, something.

"Fine," she said, "How are you?"

I am never sure how to answer this question. "Fine" is too big a lie. But no one has the time for details. Nor do I believe they want the details. So I usually say something like, "Okay," or "Middling," or "Surviving," depending on how well I know the person and my mood at the time.

"Fine," I say cheerfully. I'm in a hurry and it's only the middle of the day so it's not an unreasonable answer.

Except she stops me, looks at me and says, "No, really, how are you?"

So, I tell her briefly, about the pain, the difficulty of getting through an ordinary day. She listens. And then I say, "And how are you?"

She looks away, her eyes well. "I'm okay," she says. We talk. She pulls an essay on chronic pain that she has clipped from a magazine out of her purse. She hands it to me. We talk intensely, our heads close together. We talk about pain and grief and related issues. We are blocking the bread aisle. People edge around us. Finally, we laugh and prepare to leave each other. Then her eyes well with tears. She says, "The hard thing is, when my parents died, Dick and I faced it together. I always had him. Now I have to face his dying on my own." We hug and say good-bye with a special intensity.

Pain has a loud voice, and some days, it is the only voice I can hear – the multi-toned, multi-coloured, drone of pain. On such days, nothing exceeds it, not the voices of birds or the colours of the land around me or the kind and loving ideas of what to do from other people, or people saying anxiously, "I love you."

Pain also has an appetite; it takes the kindness and good intentions of other people, it takes the good advice and kindly ideas of caregivers, it takes the beauty of the world and turns it all into rage and bitterness. It devours the good along with the person in pain. It takes who I have been away. It takes me by surprise even when I know it's coming, even when I fight, tooth and nail, head and feet, pain wins. Of course it wins.

I had a car accident and then I had another car accident, both in unlikely times and places, both clearly not my fault. My head ached; I stopped sleeping; sound screamed in my ears. I went to doctors, lots of them and healers, lots of them, massage and physio and acupuncture and naturopaths. I paid them from my dwindling fund of non-working savings. The doctors offered what they had, which were drugs. They offered drugs and no diagnosis. They offered anti-depressants for the pain, opioids for the pain, anti-seizure drugs for the pain, sleeping pills to knock me out. I took them, of course I did. I was grateful for them.

I still am. I stand at my bureau at night, I measure out my handful of pills for pain and insomnia and I am immensely grateful. I lie down, in the dark, eager, too eager, for unconsciousness. I wait for it. I try too hard to relax, to sleep. Nothing more ridiculous than trying too hard to sleep. But the drugs are usually infallible and sweep me away in a few minutes.

But sometimes there is an hour of waiting, in the dark in pain. Then away into nothing. Perhaps I dream. Perhaps not. The internet says the pills block real sleep, that I need REM sleep to heal. I don't care. I am only greedy for the night, and freedom from pain. To be unconscious. Uncaring.

Every morning, I still wake with hope. Some days I get up, holding my head still, like balancing a too full mug of tea. Some mornings, I get through tea and toast and even the breakfast dishes and reading my emails before the pain starts, swelling my head, pressure from the inside, a slow fire building up from my neck, over my ears into my forehead. My head burning from the inside. There is nothing to do but push through and take pain meds. The pain meds shut down part of the central nervous system. Gradually, my head becomes a swollen lump on the top of my shoulders but the pain recedes. I can walk and talk but I'm faking it. Somewhere far away my body walks and talks but I am distant from my body and distant from my pain. Somewhere I have a body and a life. The lump on my shoulders smiles and talks for me. The noise in my ears is constant but distant now. I function. That's what I want. That's what my doctors want. Are you functional, they ask? Meaning, can you drive, make tea and toast?

After the second accident, for two months, all summer, I sat in a chair, non-functional, raging at the arbitrariness of two ridiculous car accidents that had stolen my life. Kind people came and went but I was unmanageable. Raging when the headaches came, pounding and burning my head. Not eating the food people brought and made for me. Dreaming of suicide. Suicide ideation, as the kindly therapists put it. Wishing to die in a way that wouldn't devastate my family, is how I thought of it. Drifting away on a raft in the middle of the night. Lost on the mountain and never found. Or the best, to die in my sleep. Take me, please, please, I said to death.

But death has its own strange rules and ignored me. It took the tools of my life instead. One sunny summer afternoon, while everyone had gone to the beach, death came in, lay all over my living room like a dusty blanket, like a suffocating haze; computer, dead, books, dead, kitchen, dead. I sat in my chair and panicked until I heard the voices of people coming back to be with me. Death fled, laughing, and I got up out of the chair to be alive again, to hear real voices, to see the faces of my daughters and my grandson.

But summer was soon over and people had lives and I had pain medication. I got up and got in my car and went for a drive. I had to cook. I talked myself through cooking. I decided to make cookies. I used to like baking. I would make cookies for my grandkids. I told myself every move to make. Take the eggs out of the fridge. Now put them back. Now mix. Now turn the stove on. Now put the cookies on a cookie sheet. Once the cookies were in the oven, I wandered away to the computer. Forgot about them until the smell of sugar burning warned me. For the next batch, I stood over the oven, waiting.

I made lists. I reminded myself of what to do. One thing at a time. Go to the bedroom for pills. But while in the bedroom, there were clothes to pick up. Maybe something in the closet to look for, back out to the kitchen to make tea. What had I been going to do? Yes, take pills, more pills please.

This from someone who had once not long ago flown through a day of chores, writing teaching, gardening. Who zipped from here to there, keeping track of a million details. Who never went to doctors. Illness? Ridiculous. Who had time for it?

I drove slowly and carefully, reminding myself to stay focused. I shopped, conscious of appearing busy and determined and normal. A shopper. A person with a life. And I watched myself, nagged myself, pushed myself, hated what I had become.

Determined, I tried to pick up all the dropped threads of my once far too busy life. I picked them up one by one and then pain got in the way. I sat in front of the computer, determined and pain sat between me and the screen. Some days I picked out one word at a time, set each one down, a line of words. Sometimes a paragraph. And another.

Reading came back too. I had spent a whole summer, not reading. Unthinkable. But now, finally, I could read a paragraph, then a story, then a book. Lots of books.

But no matter what I did, or how determined I was, in the afternoons, pain marched in and took over. Desperate, I went outside and walked and walked, the dog at my side. I walked, light-headed through glorious fall afternoons. My feet, far from my head, kept walking. I came home with just enough energy to fight my way through pain to make dinner. And then finally, gratefully, I could collapse into my office chair in front of the computer to watch and be distracted – watch anything – movies on YouTube, movies courtesy of the library, through every half-assed decent film on Netflix, watching the clock the whole way, wanting more than anything else, to be exhausted enough for it to be time to take the pills, be gladly unconscious, again, for another whole night.

So the fall went, and then winter. Each day, a routine dictated sternly by the limits of energy, the limits by my resistance to pain, by pain itself. When people I knew, kind loving people saw me in the library or the grocery store, they asked, "How are you?"

"Not so good," I would sometimes say.

And each one would do the same thing, step back, look me over like a purchase they didn't want, say with enthusiasm, "Well, you're looking good."

To which I would reply, "Yes, thanks."

Which gave them permission to go away, to tell people how they had seen me and I was looking good. It left me with a mouth full of words that recoiled back on me, and hit me again.

Who could pain rage to? Who could hear such crap? And why would they stay still to listen?

So, instead, we rage at each other, pain and I. It pounds nails into my head. When I read on Facebook and various list serves what other writers are up to, pain laughs. You can't do any of those things, you can't apply for that job, you can't do that tour, or go to that event. You can't do those things. You are off the rails. You are sick. You are dying. You are getting worse. You are in pain.

Pain takes away agency, control, ideas, initiative. There is my life, just over there, full of books, ideas, rational thoughts, research, teaching, walking, my garden, my horses. And here I am, caught by pain, veiled and wrapped around by my pain, cocooned, eaten, but still alive.

Pain is as truthful, in its way, as booze. And just as big a liar. It tells sly lies and it shines a light on my life in a way that nothing else has or does. A person in pain is not one person anymore --there is the person and then the pain raging inside. The pain is multi-voiced, bitter, vicious, angry. Pain, like booze, brings bitter truth with it, and even more bitter lies.

But the truth can't be spoken out loud. Who could withstand the acid voice of pain? Not me.

Who could argue with it? Pain can sweep away any argument, any soothing help. The voice of pain is a voice screaming for help and screaming despair. Who would even want to be in the same room, in the same vicinity as pain. The person living with it only wants to escape but there is no door, not even a crack for that fabled light.

Distraction, say the soothing caregivers. Exercise. Interrupt the cycle of pain and depression and despair. Reward yourself. Pain can be managed, interrupted, distracted, made plastic. Neuroplasticity. Change your thinking. Be positive.

Yes, I think, there is my reward, one more step towards life over there...my books, my writing, my students, my friends, ideas, things to read, understand, think about. And there are my friends, waiting to be asked to go to lunch or come for a visit. There is my kitchen, full of recipes and baking pans.

And I could, I will get up, take pain like a cage strapped to my head, balance it on my shoulders, walk to the kitchen, peer through the bars, read recipes, get out flour and milk and eggs, make something. Sometimes I do just that and sometimes it makes me feel better. Distracted. Busy. Rewarded. And when I sit down or lie down, the pain is still there.

Pain limits what I can do. But what I do is my identity -- there is panic as this slides away. I must do this, I think. I am a writer, I work with words, I read, I edit. Instead, I wander around the fringes of writing, an essay perhaps, or a manuscript that needs work. A manuscript with a hole in the story that I can't fix. I read it over and over and the words won't fall into place, the sense of it won't come. Slow, I think, go slow.

It would be easy here to fall into the pit. I can see the pit and I can hear its temptations: self righteousness (you don't understand how it feels); bitterness (this isn't my fault, why is this happening to me); fuck it, (I am so sick I am just going to hurt/kill myself, drink, take more drugs, eat too much, or whatever else self-destructive behaviours will hurry this process along); self-pity, (I am in the worst pain anyone has ever had and I need everyone around me to know it.); or other variations of this pit.

This is very similar to the pit that I used to fall into on a fairly regular basis from anxiety and depression. I always had reasons for the anxiety and depression; I was too busy, too poor, too lonely, too overworked, to pushed, too stressed. Now for the first time in my life, I'm not too busy. Instead I am in pain.

Except, there is no question that pain brings depression along with it, that physical pain and emotional pain are intertwined in ways that medicine and people in pain don't always understand. So expecting someone in pain to be cheerful is a double issue; they can't be cheerful because they are in pain...but part of pain is not being cheerful. How to win at this particular iron toothed contradiction?

"Winning", curiously enough, if winning is even close to the right word, seems to involve a certain amount of grimly determined cheer, a certain amount of exercise, a certain amount of whatever gives you joy, whether that is family or drugs, and a lot of rest and recovery. And balance between that exercise and rest and recovery. None of this easy and there is no guarantee of relief from pain. So a certain amount of sheer strength of character and will and determination comes in as well. And whatever will back up that strength of character. Prayer? Bring it on! Positive thinking, fine. Massage. Alternative healing shamans? Yes, I'll take it, I'll try it, provided it isn't dangerous or costs too much.

Sometimes healing comes by accident. Sometimes it comes when you aren't even noticing. I walked myself out of arthritis pain over a period of ten years by just that, walking and having a life. My dog walked me, my work walked me, my busy life walked me and the arthritis pain lifted and went away. I don't know if this head pain will do that. It's ten times better than it was four months ago and a hundred times better than it was last summer. But every afternoon still, an iron noose tightens around my head and squeezes my mind down into a nub of itself until I give up, insert what is left of myself into a movie, and desperately hope for distraction until bedtime and those beloved pills. Time alone will keep telling this story.

I get through each day one at a time. I do the dishes. I make the bed. Chaos waits just outside that routine. Put things in place, in order, or I will never find them again. Dementia wiggles its crooked ancient fingers. Packing for a trip, I get everything in order and then entirely forget to pack pants. Or another day, I write all morning with what energy I have and find out it was the old version of the manuscript and it all has to be redone.

My computer dies and I have no money for another one but I have to get one anyway. I am a writer. It's what I do. I need at least the tools of a writer, books, reading, a computer where words go in the keyboard and books emerge. Or they used to.

So my days continue, with moments of brightness when I emerge with energy from my mornings, determined to continue, to be me. Moments when I retreat, defeated, into darkness and the small relief of movies.

And moments when someone says, "No, really how are you, "and the pain flows into a bright electric path, lights up the connection between two people, shared words, shared understanding, however brief. I walk every day. I notice the birds, the leaves, the horses, the dog running, the black kitten at my heels. I notice I am alive. I keep on noticing, I say sometimes, to someone, "How are you," and a bright silver line of words flows between us. "Yes, I know," we say to each other, "Yes, yes I understand."

Riptide

Barbara Stahura, CJF

In my favourite photo of us, we're astride Ken's BMW motorcycle in our Tucson driveway. Ken is laughing at the camera as I, sitting behind him with arms clasped around his waist, kiss his ear. We wore none of our usual protective equipment—full-face helmets, boots, jackets, gloves—because we had jumped on the bike strictly for the photo. Months later, in December 2003, Ken was wearing all his gear when he took his other motorcycle, a Ducati sport bike, to run some errands. But when a white sedan turned suddenly in front of him, there was nothing he or his equipment could do to prevent what happened next. Ken hit the passenger side near the back wheel; helmet striking steel, face smashing into helmet, brain slamming into skull. He crashed to the asphalt. The sedan disappeared.

An injury to the brain is unlike any other. Along with physical functions, the brain controls awareness, personality, temperament, and cognitive processes like memory—all those things that comingle to form a "self." And while that self does not necessarily reside in the brain, the brain is the part of us that animates it. So a traumatic brain injury can kidnap the dear self of someone you love, dragging him far from shore as a riptide does a swimmer, sometimes beyond rescue, even though in reality he is holding your hand or smiling at you across the dinner table.

The day of the accident, exactly nine months after our wedding, Ken left around noon and had planned to be home in a couple of hours. Instead, I found myself at the University of Arizona Medical Center's ICU around 7 p.m., staggered by the sight of my husband. There was a ventilator tube in his mouth; a cervical collar around his neck; a stitched cut above his left eyebrow; left eye purple and swollen shut, right eye nearly so; nostrils filled with crusted blood; broken right hand captured in a sling; left hand tethered to the bed rail. Naked under a single sheet and his face streaked with dirt, Ken moaned and tossed in delirium.

A CT scan showed two minimal contusions on Ken's brain. The neurologists told me worse injuries invisible to imaging machines were likely. The brain floats within the skull, and if the head's momentum stops suddenly, as Ken's did when it came to an instant halt against the car, the brain rebounds within its bony home in a motion called *coup contrecoup*. Neurons are sheared off: Millions of connections in that tiny, internal universe can, like exploding stars, blink out of existence in an instant.

That Ken had suffered a traumatic brain injury (TBI) became apparent when he could talk again, four or five days after the collision. Much of his speech consisted of parroting words in a sing-song voice. After developing aspiration pneumonia, he tried to cough but couldn't cough deeply enough for relief. Smiling at him and stroking his forehead, I said, "Bummer." He sang back, "Bummer, bummer, bummer," much as a toddler would.

Next, he began repeating nonsense phrases. The first was, "Happiness is, happiness is," in a gentle rhythm. I added, "Happiness is a warm puppy," which he chanted for a while and gradually transformed to "Happiness is a warm country."

But as Ken began to speak in complete sentences, I grew more alarmed.

"I have to rewire your circuitry so I can manage you better," he told me in all delusional sincerity. He claimed his staid, seventy-seven-year-old parents were members of a steel drum band; no, wait, a plastic drum band. He insisted he had to get up and care for his patients (he's a software engineer) and that Scott, his chiropractor, repaired his motorcycles. One night, when he couldn't even sit up without help, he somehow clambered over the bed rail, wandered down the hall, and fell, hitting his head. Fortunately, he incurred no further injury. The nurse who called me said he kept repeating, "I have to find the motion. My wife and I have to find the motion." He didn't know where he was or what was happening. Even worse, he didn't know that he didn't know—a very bad sign.

After this incident, Ken was placed in a Vail bed, a mesh-sided, enclosed bed that zips from the outside. Much better than putting him in restraints, the nurse told me. Ken's short-term memory also had been damaged. He recognized everyone who came to visit but for weeks could not recall that anyone but me ever had. His speech therapist hung signs in his room as memory aids: "I was in a motorcycle vs. car accident on December 29" and "My wife's name is Barbara." She also started a memory book for him, to which I added photos of our wedding, his kids, our house, and our cat, along with affirmations proclaiming good health and normal life.

During the first few weeks, even though Ken carried on long—if sometimes weird and oddly chatty—conversations, he never really engaged with anyone. He spoke animatedly, but his gaze was distant, unconnected. Although physically in the room, he was not present; he existed in some inward place, unable to transcend the damage to his frontal lobes.

His rehab team warned me that impulse control is often a casualty of TBI, and Ken was no exception. Still weak and in danger of falling, he moved too quickly for safety. He gobbled his food. I became a nag, perhaps too protective but terrified of another injury. I reminded him again and again to slow down, be careful. Stubbornly, he refused, brushing away my concern like a pesky fly. Once, I cried in frustration, fearful that he would choke on huge forkfuls of dinner. He simply looked past me with distant eyes and continued bolting his food.

A month after the accident, Ken developed a pulmonary embolism and was transferred from rehab to an acute care hospital. One morning, he called me from there. "I don't know where I am," he whispered. "I think I've been kidnapped by foreign nationals." I stood in our kitchen, phone to my ear, stunned. Just yesterday, he had sounded so normal again. Where was the man who had looked so intensely into my eyes as he said, "I do"? Smart, articulate, an enthusiastic reader, an excellent computer programmer and woodworker, the real Ken had disappeared, replaced by someone who looked just like him but was missing essential ingredients. Should I have applied for his Social Security disability, as his case manager had advised? Would I forever be his caregiver, exhausted, frightened, and missing him?

I wanted more than anything to look inside Ken's brain, to see what the scanning machines could not, to find his lost self among the blasted neurons and bring him home. I researched TBI on the Internet, read books about it, and found many chilling and many encouraging stories about survivors. I pestered Ken's doctors and therapists with questions—Would Ken's brain heal? How much? When? —but of course, no one could provide the answers. There was nothing to do but move through the days.

When a reason for hope appeared, I clung to it—the first time Ken hugged me, remembered our phone number and called me at home, recalled a visit from neighbours the night before. And when hope lagged, I read reminders I'd hung around our house: "Relentlessly Optimistic."

Two days before his homecoming, my husband made an omelette– perfect and golden– just as he used to make for us every Sunday. All by himself. It was part of his occupational therapy. I took photos, the last one showing Ken standing in the rehab kitchen, proudly displaying his creation. We ate it for lunch. Later that day, he couldn't remember the word "omelette."

Nine months post-accident, Ken still fights headaches and fatigue, and fears he'll always be wobbly on his feet. His memory is better, although the right word often eludes him, but he still wrestles with once-easy tasks, thanks to damaged cognitive functions. He has sold his two remaining motorcycles, returned to work, and vows he won't abandon himself or me by giving up. Nearly released from the riptide, my husband, resolute and a little scared, struggles to free himself for good. When we vacationed along the Pacific Ocean, we walked the beach every day. I watched Ken cheering the surfers cresting their waves, and I silently cheered him, praying his determination would be enough to return him all the way to shore.

More than a decade after the accident, Ken has recovered remarkably well. He was able to return to shore, thanks to his great determination and many other factors, for which we are deeply grateful. We are involved in our local brain-injury community and do what we can to raise public awareness of the growing silent epidemic of traumatic brain injury.

This essay originally appeared in the Jan.-Feb. 2005 issue of Science & Spirit magazine.

David's Story

Dawn L. Metcalf

The anvil in my stomach weighs dread. As I intensely watch the scrub-dressed woman at the information desk mouth the words "Trauma Unit", I become aware of the buzzing, pulsating ring in my ears, so loud I can barely hear anything as the blood hits my eyes, jacking up my blood pressure. Nodding, I turn and run, sporadic as I dodge these damn sick and not sick people. Move damn it! I smell like fear and shock, the evidence in sour breath and dry mouth, stress odour wafting from my armpits, worry excreting from my brow and upper lip.

My nephew, that joyful, high spirited, fun-loving, sweet, gorgeous adolescent, whose smile makes young and old women's knees weak, has been terribly hurt, we'll know in the next twenty-four hours how hurt. I see a trauma nurse and ask urgently and loudly, "Where's David Braithwaite?" The nurse points to a private but open room to her right. I run again avoiding gurneys, nurses and other uniformed entities before abruptly stopping in the doorway. Assaulted by the sight and smell of blood, I watch the purposeful bustling, frantic, frenetic motion of oh-so-many young, how-can-they-possibly-know-enough nurses and doctors whose names and faces I would never know or remember. The masked angels whose day-in, day-out experience is too often spent with the awfulness and tragedy of life. Of course they will save him.

David lies on a gurney in the centre of a large treatment room with real walls, not curtains, equipment, hoses, plugs and needles connecting him to hope. The sheet absorbs the blood escaping from his ears and other wounds and the brown, sour smelling coffee ground vomit. He struggles to sit up, vaguely conscious that he is fighting desperately to live. The thick leather straps anchoring his head, arms and legs making what he said he would do after falling forty-five feet to challenge a concrete floor impossible. After impact, we were told David yelled, "I'm going home," automatically lifting and throwing the fifty foot steel ladder that fell with him, twenty-five feet away. If the impact doesn't kill, violence is often the head's reaction to blunt-force trauma. He violently refused unconsciousness, requiring his coworkers to subdue him until the ambulance arrived. David is built like a tank, a scouted, talented hockey player, an enforcer. Add these qualities to the raw violence of a head injury and it would be like wrestling a grizzly.

The boy on the stretcher didn't resemble David at all. This boy's face was so swollen, broken and bloody, his eyes forcibly closed by tightly stretched skin containing fluids that came from God only knows where. His struggle amazed and saddened me to a depth I didn't know possible. "Oh my God, David" is all I could think, my eyes welling, the anvil sinking deeper.

Scanning the room I saw my sister and brother-in-law standing on the right side of the room, a short distance from their son, eyes red and swollen, holding back emotion lest pain and fear crumble them to the floor to speak nonsense, gaining admission to a locked ward away from their son. I saw the mix of pain and terror. Frozen, they stared at their son. In another setting the blankness might have been mistaken for disinterest, but this was shock and grudging acceptance that they could do nothing but wait. They had surrendered to the angels, watching them hover, measure, talk, whisper, inject and test their boy.

I walked over to my sister and wrapped my arms around her. The rigidity of her watching ceased as she released herself to me, shoulders heaving as she sobbed. After a time, the shuddering stopped. Breathing deep she wiped her eyes then clasped her hands just under her breasts as if in prayer. She wasn't praying. Long ago I recognized it as the way she stands or sits when she's afraid. She was very afraid that day, afraid of losing the soft boy whose nature is closest to hers. Knowing I might be rejected, I felt compelled to try and connect with and embrace my brother-in-law, the man I had known since I was ten years old. In 1965, we had moved from Winnipeg to Langley and he was the fourteen-year-old boy living across the street. I was the new girl in the neighbourhood and even before he met my sister, he protected me from the boy bullies, setting his blonde Labrador on them when they chased me home from the school bus stop. But he turned away. I knew why. His grief and fear would find release safely alone with my sister, where emotional collapse wouldn't signify weakness. This intimacy was theirs, not mine. I respectfully looked into his eyes, nodded, patted his back and returned to my sister. We exited the room to talk. Her voice shaky she explained that they were waiting to hear what happened. Someone told her that the site dispatcher dialed 911 as soon as Dave started falling and that the ambulance was really fast to arrive.

We would find out just how fast later. "They don't know if he'll make it," she cried, adding, "They said that it's a good sign that he hasn't lost consciousness, that if he stays awake he has a chance."

After speaking with my sister I called our father who had stayed home with my daughter. I felt guilty that I had asked him to watch her. He should be with us. He has a right to be with his grandson. I apologized to him and offered to come home so he could go to the hospital, but he said that he was ok, that I was to stay, but to phone him with updates. I'm not sure, but I don't think he could bear the possibility of losing his only grandson or witness his pain. His wife, our mother, passed away six months earlier - we had watched her slowly lose her struggle to live. We were grieving her loss, trying to re-centre the family and now we might lose David. I could hear anguish in his voice as he softly uttered, "Ah, geez."

Returning to the trauma room, I saw an entirely different set of nurses and doctors talking to each other, reading charts, checking lines and heart rates. I walked over to David and leaning close to his right ear said, "We're here Dave. We love you and we want you to fight like hell. Don't go to sleep David. Please don't go to sleep." He didn't sleep for a long time. He fought like hell.

Hours passed without registering. Drinking cup after cup of bitter coffee, we paced and waited. Licking our fingers to flip through old scrubby magazines, we didn't care whose grimy, germy hands had previously handled them.

Sometime during the vigil, we received information about what had happened. David's boss asked the crew who wasn't afraid of heights. David, an eager eighteen year old, raised his hand. Without safety training or gear, he had been told to get up to the ceiling heating ducts. The ducts gave way hurtling him to the floor. His co-workers reported that they found blood on walls fifty feet away from where he landed. A terrible impact.

X-rays revealed multiple fractures to the bottom or basal area of David's skull and right arm, broken cheeks and shattered right hand. The jarring of the landing caused every joint in his body to shift and his teeth were loose. Doctors would rebuild his right hand, but they couldn't rebuild his brain. He suffered a severe brain injury; doctors eventually reporting that he lost eleven percent of function and that his short term memory was severely impaired or completely gone. Time would reveal the truth.

We were relieved and grateful when we knew David survived the first twenty-four hours. I was also humbled. I witnessed the energy and will he mustered to stay when he could easily have drifted away. I thought of my troubles and realized that as difficult as my life had turned out to be, compared to what my nephew was facing in the coming months and years, my life was ok. My physical being, especially my brain, was intact. I was terrified to even consider the limitations and frustration a damaged brain imposes. I would be there for my sister and my nephew.

Finally allowed to sleep, but not without interruption, David began his restorative journey. Once they were confident that he was stable and capable of tolerating the anesthetic, doctors rebuilt his hand and set his arm. His cheeks and skull fractures would heal on their own, in time. His arm and hand elevated and in casts, aided by drugs that suspend time and space, he slept, irritable if visitors or nurses stole his slumber to talk, test, or, well, do anything. On my first ward visit, I noticed his meal tray sitting where it had been delivered, untouched and cold. Pushing aside an orange, I lifted the stainless steel cover to reveal a slab of overcooked roast beef and some grayish looking potatoes and carrots. Food sweat ran down the inside of the stainless steel cover landing like transparent gravy on the tired looking meal. Even if he were capable of eating, he couldn't cut the beef or potatoes and certainly couldn't peel an orange. The insensitivity of this infuriated me. I cut his food into bite size pieces and tried feeding him, but he lacked interest. First of all, his teeth weren't up to the task and second, he couldn't and didn't want to interact. His concussed brain, bruised and swollen, shunted to drain fluid was heavily tasked with repairing itself. Many different nurses monitored him regularly and closely. Swelling was the enemy, which, if it should present at dangerous levels, demanded surgery to release the pressure.

A few days went by before he awoke for increasing amounts of time. Confused, he thankfully had no memory of the fall. Although we knew his short-term memory was compromised we didn't know or accept that it was gone, at least for now. Obviously the brain is hyper complex, the degree and rate of recovery varying greatly from person to person. Doctors told my sister that it would take at least two years before the permanence of the damage could be assessed. There was hope. We would deal with the memory loss, but were totally unprepared for the loss of the personality we had watched grow from a tiny baby, to a cute as a button little boy, to the strong, vital young man my nephew had become.

David was in the hospital for one week. His discharge signified the beginning of a new and very different life. Plans were made and therapies designed to restore his strength and rebuild his life. In the first few months after his release, we became aware of some age inappropriate behaviours, especially in the way he expressed his sense of humour. His social skills seemed to have regressed about six years. What I noticed were his eyes. Although his body displayed correct reactions to emotion, his eyes were vacant. I had seen this look in the eyes of a severely brain injured man I knew in the community and my heart sank because I knew the man had acquired severe health issues stemming from his loss of impulse control with food and alcohol and that he was socially isolated having few, if any, true friends. I worried for David. Although he tried to be himself - his old self - he couldn't manage it. When he became aware of the difference, he began grieving his own death, the death of his old self. It was heartbreaking but in reality, to us, his loss didn't register in the same magnitude as it did to him. To us, he was alive and that's all that mattered. We celebrated his survival. To him, the changes were both physically and emotionally catastrophic. He wasn't sure of anything anymore, especially of his own being, who he was and what he might be. He had planned to become a millwright, but school was no longer in his future. All David ever wanted from life was to work at something he enjoyed, something that allowed him to provide for a family. Although David's dreams were not big in the grandiose sense, they were honourable and spoke volumes about his character.

David was born in New Westminster, but raised in Prince George. He had returned to Vancouver to work and save money for school. At the time of his accident he was earning seven dollars an hour. In 1989, the WCB lifetime disability pension was awarded at the wage earned at the time of the accident. There was no legal recourse. WCB prohibits injured parties to file civil actions no matter how unjust the circumstances. Knowing my sister was very tired and not overly familiar with bureaucratic processes, I became her sounding board and advisor. Having worked for government in an administrative and quasi-official capacity in the past, I had learned the dance, how to approach and navigate the loopholes, what would guarantee attention, interest and sympathy. I passed on this information to her, assessing the experts assessments and strategizing on her next moves and remarks. At the end of a very long process of assessment from doctors and practitioners and the development of a positive relationship between my sister, David and the WCB counsellor, it was determined that because David was registered in the millwright program at a local college at the time of the accident he would receive a life time pension equivalent to the considerable salary level of a millwright. The pension would be indexed and exempt from claims resulting from divorce or other legal proceedings, and if he could one day work again, his pension would not be compromised or jeopardized. He was now financially safe, but still at risk emotionally.

Dave's injury fractured the family dynamic, challenging my sister's marriage, the relationship between David and his sister, and my sister and brother-in-law's relationship with their daughter. Observers could only speculate about what they were dealing with on any given day. David had changed, but slowly a new Dave emerged as my sister and brother-in-law re-raised the man-boy through a second and very different adolescence. Rebuilding the foundation of a personality caught between past and present is extremely stressful, balancing between assumptions about what he understood and what he didn't, hoping not to insult or embarrass him. Stress overwhelmed David; he was highly sensitive to situations and people he no longer had the confidence to deal with. He leaned heavily on his mother for emotional support and to 'talk him down'.

Life has not been easy for Dave. Some things that are easy to most people aren't easy or possible for him. But where lesser people might have given up, he hasn't. He has developed into a good man, who over time, has learned to trust that many of his dreams could come true. Shortly after the accident, David returned to Prince George because his long-term memory of the Prince George streets was solid and he could drive without getting lost. As the years passed, David learned about his capabilities and limitations through both triumph and defeat. He has been fired from jobs because the positions required too much from his short term memory and hired and respected for the quality of work he produces when given tasks not involving too much reasoning or stress. As soon as he could, he returned to lifting weights and working out at the gym, rebuilding his strength and size. Aware that one more concussion could put him out for good, he chose life, not merely existence, playing a game of hockey now and then, eventually coaching his young son's team.

David has learned and relearned life's basic operations, becoming physically, emotionally and financially independent. He has loved and had his heart broken a couple of times. Finding a relationship that can stand the test of time isn't easy for people without head injuries, but even rarer for those with one. The pool of women enlightened enough to take on a man without a short term memory, at risk of further brain damage, and who, as doctors predicted, would suffer from his injuries after the age of forty, is small.

David's first marriage produced two children. After re-marrying, he fought for and was eventually awarded custody of his children. His second wife loves him deeply. They became a family of six. His wife's youngest child has Down's syndrome. A lovely girl, she and David are very close. He often smiles and jokingly says, "I kinda relate to her."

Years ago, after purchasing their home, David added a massive addition to ensure enough room for their soon-to-be teenagers and a kennel from which to breed and sell English Bulldogs. He was mid-husband during Daisy's deliveries and rescued pups during difficult labours. I've heard it said that owners often come to resemble their pets. Well, David does remind me of a bulldog. He is brave, courageous and gentle, without the under bite and the drooling. At forty-three, he is a handsome man, his face long ago healed and unscarred. He indeed began feeling the long term physical effects of the accident around forty. He has adjusted what he does for work, but he hasn't quit.

David glued the pieces of a broken mirror back together and although the image is not the original, it's better than enough. A line from the 2003 movie Seabiscuit says it all when trainer Tom Smith (played by Chris Cooper), spoke of the horse's value saying, "You don't throw a whole life away just 'cause it's banged up a little." Like Seabiscuit, David, with time, training and support, became a champion.

My Last Game of Hockey

Alastair Larwill

I chipped the puck past the defenseman and broke over the blue line. Things were going great that game, I had bagged myself a goal and I was playing well. A quick side step around this big guy and I should be away to the races. I lean in and reach to get control of the puck, a shadow, solid impact, sideways, on the ice.

Where did he come from? I slowly get up, another guy is on the ground, not the same guy I chipped the puck past.

"Sorry man," he says as I skate away.

The ice is more sideways then usual as I curl to get back in the play; my team mate is losing his shit on the bench. This doesn't feel right, so I cross over and go to the bench. I sit down and try and relax, I look across the ice and it's moving like a typewriter back and forth. Hmmm, I don't think I can finish this game. I look for the key to the dressing room, tell my team mate, "I'm done man," wait for the play to stop and go get changed.

It takes me what feels like ten minutes to unlock the door. As I change, I wonder if I should drive or not. We're at Vanier Arena which is close to my place so it should be alright. Maybe I shouldn't drive, but I don't really have much choice do I?

I get home alright, my girlfriend is asleep and I wonder if I should go to a doctor, I'll probably take tomorrow off to be safe; walking up the stairs was kind of trippy. I text my boss to give her a heads up on what happened. She replies asking how I am. I say that I should be alright.

The next morning I get up and I feel okay, but when I walk it feels like I'm on a rocky ship swaying back and forth. When I open the bedroom door I feel like I narrowly avoid walking into it. I hold the railing as I walk down the stairs. My girlfriend is up and I tell her, "I think I've been concussed." She flips out and ensures I make an appointment with the doctor. I tell her that I'm going to relax this weekend, take it easy and I should be fine by Monday. What is a doctor going to do? Tell me to rest, relax and take it easy.

I spend most of the weekend under a blanket listening to the TV. It's funny because the TV doesn't do the typewriter thing as much as looking at objects do, but it gives me more of a headache.

My girlfriend asks if I'm okay when I hide under the blanket and I tell her I'm fine. Which is mostly true, I'm fine under the blanket, but not otherwise. I rest, I relax, I take it easy.

Monday rolls around and I have an audit first thing. When I get out of bed, the world is still on a boat, but I can manage it. I load up my car and drive to the assessment. Driving seems to be alright, okay, I can do this. I park and introduce myself to my client. I tell her that I might take a little longer today because I had an incident last week playing hockey. We fill out the paper work and I explain that I will change her light bulbs and meter her fridge to help her save money on her electricity bills. I love working for my company, it helps low income people reduce their consumption to help the planet and their bottom line.

I pull out the fridge with relative ease, sometimes the fridges stick to the floor, but not this time and I put the meter on it. Great, we are rolling; let's start with the kitchen lights.

"Do you know how many incandescent light bulbs it takes to use more electricity then a TV?" I ask her. She says, "I don't know."

"Take a guess it's between one and ten," I say as I fold out my ladder and grab the CFL lights I am going to swap the incandescent for.

"Eight," she says.

I step up on the ladder, look up, take the light fixture, look down. "Woah," I say as the world starts to swirl again. I hold onto the ladder and relax for a moment, "It's two," I say as an effort to save face and then change the lights. I get down off the ladder and say, "I'm going to have difficulty today, more then I expected. I'm feeling dizzy."

She sits me down and gives me some juice. After a couple minutes of rest and a little chat with the lady, I go back to changing lights. It's a slow process and I probably shouldn't have done it, but I come from a background of soldiering on through and getting the job done. It's one assessment, it was only around ten lights, but I knew that it was too much for me.

Call the boss, call the doctor, and sit in my car until things calm down. Drive home and listen to the TV, it's remembrance day.

Later I see my doctor. I tell her what happened and that I've had a couple concussions before, I had my teeth knocked out in grade nine, and I got a concussion sometime during high school, yes playing hockey, I also had one when I hit my head on the safety bar of a scissor lift, but that is another story.

I tell my doctor that this one feels really different, after the scissor lift one I was given a week of light duty work and no ladders and I was fine.

She tells me that I am concussed and that I have to take a week off and then I should come back and get reassessed. She tells me to relax, not to watch TV or play video games, and not to exercise or anything like that.

A very long and boring week passes, I listen to a fair amount of TV, I sleep a lot. Every morning is the same though; I live in a house that is on the sea and it teeters back and forth.

The next Monday, I am frustrated, nothing has changed, I've done nothing and nothing is happening. I explain my symptoms again to my doctor and that it's not like the times before. She says the impact sounded like it was significant, and that I was making good progress, but I am going to have to take another week off.

I felt terrible, I ask her for a couple notes and I bring them into the office. I meet with my boss and my boss's boss. I tell them that I still can't go back to work, that I am progressing slowly, and that I still don't have my full facilities back. They are extremely understanding; I have always proven to be a hard worker and they understand how much working does mean to me. Fundamentally I like to help people and this is basically all what my job requires me to do.

It's a frantic week, it passes so slowly, I'm stressed that I'm not going to be normal again, that I'm always going to be nauseous after meals. What do you do when you can't do anything? Nothing, and nothing takes longer to accomplish then something, because you can't see your progress.

I keep looking up when ever I stand up and I am so nervous about hitting my head on an open cupboard door.

But progress is made; I watch a movie about midway through the week. It's Bronson, a movie about Britain's most famous prisoner. I empathize with him because I feel like I am imprisoned in my own home, imprisoned in my wavy head that is allergic to light.

I like the movie because I appreciate how good I've got it. I'm not in jail for life, I have prospects, I have a job that loves me and will wait for me. I've got it good, and I just watched a movie with only one break to relax my head.

Next Monday I bring my girlfriend to the doctor. I have an emotional break down, I cry like a child, it sort of washes over me. It happens when I explain my feelings of letting everybody at work down. It's uncontrollable, it happens and I just have to quickly cry it out. My doctor asks if people are telling me that and I tell her "No, it's just how I feel."

My doctor explains that I am in fact making progress, large progress. She says that being able to watch TV with little breaks, and having moments of stability means that I am on the mend. This also means that these dizzy spells are probably going to go away. She even suggests that I could start working here and there a little, for an hour or two, but stresses not to push it.

I start back at work little by little. My bosses are understanding and this makes a huge difference in my ability to relax; I like getting out of the house to see my co-workers and to do something productive. I'm allowed to take short walks, but cautioned not to push it. Slowly I get back to my old life.

I quit hockey… and I miss it.

I saw a team mate over Christmas; we talk about what happened because he wasn't at that game. We've both had our bells rung a couple of times and he tells me that it's probably for the best that I duck out of hockey. Concussion can lead to a higher chance of mental illness, depression, Parkinson's disease, and memory loss and Alzheimer's. I tell him, "The human mind is an amazing thing and the human body heals itself." I leave the party knowing that he's right, the statistics and research are there to prove it, but that doesn't matter because it can't help me.

I believe in pataphysics. It is the exercise of using imaginary solutions to real life problems. Imaginary solutions are the best type of solutions when no other solutions are available. Everyday I am getting better, and my mind is weaving new pathways. Every challenge is an exercise for my brain to improve itself.

Don't let disturbing signs direct your path, but take small steps towards the future in which you want to live. And there are signs, taking little things at work too personally, creeping feelings of anxiety that everything will be taken away randomly with out notice. These are bad signs, but they are not stop signs, they are warning signs, be careful, be cautious. Don't let those signs be direction signs; you direct your own life through the chaos that is this world. In a year's time, "big" problems turn out to be little stepping stones on your path to a better life.

Your brain is in your hands; use the love of your family and friends to shape it.

Our Lady of Perpetual Surprise:
Reflections of a Recovered Concussive

Meg Stainsby

We're on a road trip and Nova Scotia beckons, so I'm loading the car. From North Cable Head, we'll drive west to peek at Green Gables, criss-cross the island province again to take the Wood Islands ferry back over the Northumberland Strait. Only a few more bags to load, cousins to kiss and we're off. All but the road snacks and wet beachwear are stashed as I repeat my steps between cottage and car. I open the rented Pontiac Sunfire's rear door, lean in, place my cargo on the seat. As I pull back, righting myself, *whack!* I'm slugged in the right temple by the return swing of the door—clipped by its protruding metal edge. I'm knocked against the cab, momentarily dazed but not out.

"Ow!"

Nobody hears. I shake my head, touch the spot already swelling—no blood— and return indoors for the last bag of food.

As we drive away, I use a frozen juice box as an ice pack, driving with one hand, holding the juice ice-cube to my throbbing temple, as long as I can bear, with the other. A headache's coming, but the injury hardly seems memorable— certainly not catastrophic. By afternoon, driving south from Truro to Halifax, I should have forgotten it altogether.

But I don't forget. That evening I'm overtaken by the first symptoms of concussion, diagnosed two days later by an emergency-room doctor in Lunenburg, NS. He predicts headaches and dizziness for up to six months; however, my symptoms fail to resolve and I'm moved, medically speaking, to the more exclusive category of concussion patients whose symptoms do not abate so quickly, possibly not at all. For nearly three years, my life will be defined by this injury, variously called mild traumatic brain injury, acquired traumatic brain injury, closed head injury, eventually post-concussive syndrome.

❦   ❦   ❦   ❦

At the time of my injury, in 2004, I was forty-one, a single mother of two girls (eleven and fourteen). By profession, I was an instructor of English literature and writing; in my spare time, I'd just completed a second Master's degree, overseen a major renovation to my seventy-five year-old farmhouse, and had a one-act play produced in a student theatre festival. The trip to the Maritimes came at the end of an extraordinarily busy school year, and offered the girls and me an unheard-of seventeen days together, uninterrupted by their sojourns with their father.

My early writings reveal that the first months post-injury were a time of complex deficits, as many of my cognitive functions and emotional responses simply vanished. Here are the biggies. I lost creative thought—meaning access to my dream life, to metaphor and symbolism; to my capacity to think by association and analogy; and to my own creative work. Two or three weeks post-injury, I began losing my short-term memory, and shortly thereafter, went off work. I lost my appetite for fiction and poetry, switching to non-fiction. My affect flattened. I lost my sense of lightness—humour, playfulness, wit. Early on, I lost my will, my capacity to formulate or pursue desires other than basic ones (to eat and sleep).

Then that shifted: I became impetuous, acting without reflection or regard for consequence. I lost the highly-activated chatterbox who lived inside my head, prodding me on to multi-task, to anticipate, to chart my way through life as a high-functioning woman. I lost the neurotic shadow-side to this confident chatterbox—the anxious second-guesser who reflected compulsively on my actions, motivations, words. I lost some aspects of empathy, what I prefer to call my emotional imagination—that intuitive grasp of how others will feel in response to what I do or say. I lost an awareness of time passing. Partly because of this, because I lost interest in social interaction and because I wasn't permitted to drive after dark, I fell out of touch with friends. And even though there was a brighter side—my decade-long battle with insomnia disappeared, as did some excess weight—these losses meant that intellectually, emotionally, socially, creatively, I was changed.

The loss most obvious to people around me was of my short-term memory. This emerged early post-trauma. A simple example: one September morning, I sat down in front of email. Still in my pyjamas, the idea of tea just forming in my mind, I heard the kettle whistle in the kitchen. The girls had slept at their dad's, so this surprised me. In the kitchen, I found that, *ta-da!*, someone else had already had that very same thought about tea. I turned off the stove and poured myself a pot-full. Of course, I deduced that the other person must have been me (clever me), but try as I might, I couldn't recall having already gone through the water-boiling steps. Even faced with such concrete proof as a steaming mug of Red Rose, my mind was blank. No "*Ah, yes!*" moment. And this became a pattern: someone or something would force me to recognize that I had had yet another memory lapse, but even the clear *fact* of the lapse did nothing to "remind" me of whatever information I had failed to retain. My most common expression in these early weeks was "*Oh!*" I was becoming Our Lady of Perpetual Surprise.

At our next appointment, my doctor administered some common short-term memory and cognitive function tests. These revealed another major deficit, one more threatening to my sense of self than my failure to encode or recall information. First, I was asked to count backwards from one hundred by intervals of seven. As a former grade 4 math champ, I wouldn't have thought this could be tricky, but because I couldn't hang onto the number that resulted from one subtraction while turning my attention to the next, it was tricky indeed. When I asked the doctor how I'd performed, she said, "Not too badly."

But the real failure came next, when she gave me one minute to name as many mammals as I could. I'd love to know what a healthy-brained person comes up with. Twenty? Thirty? I named eight: rabbit, dog, cat, horse, bear and three more, again forgotten. Then I just sat, silent, aware that I was conducting a mental search but unable to reach after the missing words. The search seemed to take on a spatial, three-dimensional aspect: looking across my interior field of vision, I "saw" a white expanse, an undifferentiated tundra-like surface stretching into nothingness. White and empty. I thought, information is here somewhere, but I see no clues, only blank terrain. I felt that *something*, some feature on the landscape, should lead me on, but the rest of my minute ticked by fruitlessly. Finally I said, "I don't know how to find the rest of the words. I can't see any markers."

I went straight from that appointment to lunch with a friend, so I put the test to her. She not only listed way more animals (over twenty) but articulated the memory retrieval system by which she was identifying them.

"Let's see: African mammals, right? Zebra, elephant, giraffe, lion…." Then: "Cat family: tiger, panther, cougar, lynx…"

"That's it!" I broke in. "The dog *family!* That includes wolf, coyote, fox—not just dog." Such were the categories or strategies that I'd looked for in vain, strategies upon which, as a highly-associative thinker, I normally rely. Once my friend named them for me, I could use them; I just couldn't access them independently. Thinking via analogies and associations is vital to analytical and creative thinkers; it's what I've done professionally my entire adult life. Yet, with my current cognitive ability, I was a metaphoric and an associative dunce.

Soon sent off work on medical leave, I readily surrendered professional responsibilities and entered a new phase, one marked by a spirit of deep relaxation and loss of desire, of drive—no doubt helped along by my short-term memory gaps, since it's hard to be anxious about things one doesn't remember. I turned my whole attention to health and wellness, consulting a naturopath for brain-healing remedies, taking gingko and herring oil supplements, beginning a detoxification diet—giving up meat, wheat, dairy, eggs, sugar, caffeine, alcohol. (That left me with tofu—tofu and lots of rice.) I spent several afternoons swimming and steaming out impurities in the sauna. I joined a gym and began working out three times a week. I lost weight, toned up, felt metabolically efficient. I recall saying to friends that, notwithstanding the soreness lingering at my right temple and my bizarrely fluid symptoms, I felt pretty good. In many ways, better than I'd felt in years.

The ease with which I let go of habits—certain foods, coffee all morning, cider or wine most evenings—baffled yet delighted me. I've felt a need to monitor my own vices for years, to give them up occasionally just to prove to myself that I could. I know from these efforts, as from having given up cigarettes after ten years of heavy smoking, that one can long plan for abstinence and yet, faced with momentary temptation—out with friends, walking by a café—cave in, with glee. Suddenly, abstaining was a snap. I made no preparations, just looked at the restrictions on the naturopath's list, said "okay" and turned from these items on the spot. As if they were nothing. As if I had no desires to resist. For the first time as an adult, I felt free of all cravings. I noted all this not-minding, this easy asceticism, in my health journal.

The freedom—or perhaps emptiness—of life without urges seems to me to have been linked, somehow, to another loss, that of my ability to follow through on intention, to fulfill a plan of action. This wasn't universally the case: I could develop a routine such as going to the gym daily. But I experienced no *desire* to go to the gym. I would simply go because my doctor said it would be a good idea—and because someone (me?) had written "gym" on my wall calendar. I functioned most reliably when enacting deeply-engrained habits, such as buying groceries and seeing the girls off to school. When faced with one-off or occasional duties—to respond to social invitations, make or attend appointments, phone someone—my follow-through was not good. Such commitments were as forgettable as a pot of water boiling in the next room.

Car trips were prime occasions for me to lose track of intention. Inside my frontal lobe, a new idea could come along like a curling rock—and knock!—any plan I'd had shot right out of the target zone. A song on the radio could do this, even an interesting sign along the road. Driving alone, I could travel far off track—for miles!—before being recalled from my wanderings. Typically, when I "came to," I'd find myself on autopilot heading for one of the two most familiar places, the college where I'd taught for a dozen years, or the girls' school. When they were with me, though, the girls became good at monitoring my focus:

Erin: "Mum. Do you know where you're going?"

Me: [Quick look around.] "No idea."

Erin: "We're driving Michael home."

Me: [Glance in the rear-view mirror. Michael?] "Okay."

I'd pull a u-turn and head to Michael's house.

It surprises people that I characterize this time as stress-free, but without the capacity to anticipate, I felt calm (if not slightly stunned). Imagine how liberating it might be to be impervious to the sense, ever, that one ought to be doing anything. I'd become a child of the moment. Tillie and Erin certainly enjoyed some of my new *laissez-faire* attitude. My contented energy in the house contrasted sharply with the super-mummy blur that used to whiz around our kitchen on a workday afternoon, juggling phone calls, dinner prep, homework supervision, internal replay of the day, financial worries. Now, instead of pushing the girls to start their homework as soon as we got home, I could quickly become a playmate. Tillie would ask if I wanted to play a game, and I'd pause—listening, as ever, for that inner voice to tell me if I wanted anything, anything at all, anything other than what was on offer at that moment. In the absence of any reason not to, I'd drop to the floor in front of the coffee table and we'd play. We played a lot that autumn. Yahtzee! Crazy Eights. Scrabble. We'd play until Tillie asked, "Can we have dinner now?" Pause. Think. Why not? "Okay." Pliable.

About one month post-trauma, my inner accountant also either got drunk or went AWOL. Erin quickly detected my relaxed hold on money. I'd put her on a clothing budget when she turned twelve. Since then, she had chosen how to spend each monthly installment: sometimes, socks and underwear ranked high on her list; other times, two months' funds went on extravagant designer jeans. The responsibility was character-building, I thought, delighted to see how quickly she'd cottoned on to the value of clearance racks. But I could be a tough banker: if she ran out of socks while hoarding money for sexier items, then her feet went bare. I resisted many requests for an advance so she could buy something she just had to have, *right now!*

"When you get a job," I'd say, "you'll get paid when you get paid, period. Same thing here." That's the kind of mum I'd been.

Our next clothing budget conversation went more like this:

Erin: "Momma, have you thought about giving me extra money for clothes?"

Me: "Oh. No. I was supposed to think about that?"

Erin: "Mum! You said you just had to figure out why it could be okay. You've got to take me shopping—I need jeans!"

Me: "Oh, right. You do. But I don't give you money outside your clothing budget. That's why it's called a budget."

Erin: "But we talked about this! You said you'd think about it. Remember?"

Me: "Oh, okay. Yes, I think I did. But how do I justify this?"

Erin: [hand on hip, extra-arch in her eyebrow] "You know, Mum, this 'teach your daughter how to budget' game is very good and all, but sometimes you just have to clothe your children! Just because they're your children!"

Me: [laughing to the point of hiccoughs] "Okay. You win."

And because I'd lost the faculties of regret (backwards worry) and anticipation (forwards worry), I fussed no more. Erin and I hit the mall and spent an extra two hundred and fifty dollars. I enjoyed myself as much as she did.

❧ ❧ ☙ ☙

Impulsivity soon led me to begin blurting out thoughts without filter, without pause or reflection. Head-injury patients are notorious for outbursts—most often shows of anger or aggression. I recall no anger, but I certainly began to speak freely, without inhibition. I shocked a few salesclerks and bank tellers with my directness. If someone treated me gruffly, I'd look her in the eye and say, "Please don't be rude to me" as I handed her my cash. No anger, no sarcasm, but no bullshit either—and generally no self-recrimination later. I'd think, "That was unlike me" and let it go.

Some of my truths would have been better left unsaid, such as when I told a married friend that I was interested in spending more time with him and suggested dinner. Of course, I would have liked to spend more time with him—if only he hadn't been married. Before the head injury, I would have bit my tongue, understanding that my attraction to him was entirely my problem; I'd been at least as adept as the next adult at exercising good judgement (courtesy, kindness, what have you). But disinhibition led me time and again into wholly unguarded interactions—like Jim Carrey's character in *Liar, Liar,* cursed with compulsive honesty.

In those early post-concussion months, I experienced my mind as a place of unconnectedness. It was full of walls, silos, all stillness and dark where once it had been a breezy, well-lighted place, a place of sparks, of leaps and insights, of speed and fluidity, and of dazzling synaptical energy. Now, when someone put a question to me, I in turn would hand it over to my brain, like an old-fashioned telephone operator patching an incoming call to the appropriate line. I was just the middleman. The problem arose when no one picked up at the other end. (Ring, ring. Nobody home? Gee.) Just as I'd done at the doctor's, while waiting for mammal names to appear, I would experience myself in such situations as passive, waiting for my brain to hand me an opinion or answer. What do I believe? How do I feel? How does one decide for or against a request? Who was I to say?

For someone who lived professionally in language, teaching the beauty of metaphor, pattern recognition, theme and meaning, such lack of integration was profoundly alien, as if I were seeing only one colour-sliver of a refracted light beam after having lived my life awash in whiteness. I was unable to process one moment in light of any other. "What do I want?" was a question I could answer only head-on, isolated from related questions such as, *Should* I want this? Or, How would X feel if I *said* I wanted this? Such cognitive deficits challenged my sense of self not only as a professional but as a creative person, and as a friend; they threatened my Jungian's love of wholeness and my Unitarian's regard for interdependence, what I might describe as my rather ecological grasp of what it is to be human. Without access to such interconnectedness, I was off balance. And I had long since internalized the notion that being balanced was core to my identity. For me, this was radical loss of selfhood. Still, in my detached and curious way, I merely noted these changes in my journal and thought to myself, *Oh!*

My impulsivity led to another out-of-character move, one more significant than splurging on jeans or propositioning a friend. The girls then attended a specialty arts school in the historic village of Fort Langley, tucked along the Fraser River. We longed to move there—not just to eliminate my forty-five minute, twice-daily commute, but to give them a neighbourhood of friends and me the access to street life—coffee shops, bookstores, arts groups—that the Fort affords. Before my head injury, we'd occasionally visited open houses, once considered living in a too-small apartment in the one apartment block in town. Yet I'd dragged my feet at the actual prospect of moving. I hesitated out of anxiety, worried that too much change for the girls on the heels of their parents' separation would do them harm. I had come from a chaotic family myself—by the age of nine, I was living in my fifteenth home, attending my fourth school—and I felt a crippling (probably misplaced) need to compensate to the girls for their own family breakdown by staying put. Even to think about moving would release the ghosts of a childhood gone emotionally very wrong, and I'd panic. So we stayed. Luckily, I genuinely loved our farmhouse—even more since I'd renovated it, restoring old wood floors, giving myself a big, bright master bedroom. And years of landscaping work meant that the large garden now produced an annual parade of blossoms that marched steadily from February to November. Although I hated the location, remote from friends and siblings, the home itself was warm, safe. I had no intention of leaving.

Until the head injury: enter spontaneity, exit anxiety and emotional fragility. One October afternoon, Tillie and I happened to look in at the local realtor's window after school and noticed a listing for one of those too-small apartments in the village. We asked for a tour. We liked. I pulled Tillie aside:

"You won't be heart-broken to leave the house? The yard? Your new purple bedroom?"

"Nope," she said.

"Okay," I said. We walked back to his office. I wrote out an offer and signed it, then took Tillie grocery shopping, promptly forgetting what I'd done.

Sometime the next weekend, at a family Thanksgiving supper, I remembered. "We might be moving," I blurted out, *à propos* of nothing. Heads turned. "I put an offer on an apartment the other day, in Fort Langley."

My news met with surprise and concern. No one knew I'd been looking to move (I hadn't been). Hadn't I just renovated our house? (Yup.) Would the new place have as spacious a bedroom for me? (Nope.) An inspiring writing space— a study full of light and wood? (Nope. No study, in fact.) Three bedrooms, at least? (Uh, no.) Would I have anything like my lush garden to look out on? (Uh, no garden. Third floor.) Could we take our dog, cats and rabbits? (Rabbits? I forgot we had rabbits....)

In the next weeks, many people who love me fretted. Lawyer friends pointed out that I hadn't read the strata bylaws or arranged for a home inspection. The realtor's assistant called me after I missed the date for removing the subjects on the offer. (Of course I missed it: I didn't remember placing subjects....) I apologized and promptly drove to the office and removed them all—without, of course, following up on any of them. I was legally incompetent. Yet the move was on.

※ ※ ※ ※

Over late autumn 2004 and spring 2005, some of my lost mental facility would re-appear occasionally, but recovery was not linear. In the case of selling my home, my grasp of the significance of my decision lagged months behind the fact of moving. In fact, I didn't really "get" what I'd done until sometime in 2006. In the case of sending up a romantic flare to my married friend, it was three days after I invited him to dinner that I suddenly flashed on the emotional risk of expressing my attraction to him (egad! butterflies entered my tummy); at the same time, and more significantly, I grasped that I'd behaved in a way of which I didn't approve. What must he be thinking of me?

I took comfort in these insights. They were signs of recovery, however delayed, small or impermanent. In late October, my health journal notes that I woke up aware, for the first time since the whack on my temple, that I'd been dreaming. I missed my dream-life. I'd always loved falling asleep because such a wonderful world awaited me. This new night-time quiet behind my eyes was a definite bummer. Progress was erratic, though, sometimes fleeting, mixed with shifting concussion symptoms and fluctuating levels of headache and fatigue. My notes record times when Erin pointed out improvements. To her, I seemed more "normal" on days I might be quick, "snappy," capable of coming out of my fog long enough to bark out a command or grow annoyed at her forgetfulness. We'd smile at these observations, and she'd say, "Don't get better too quickly. I like Dreamy-Mummy."

As Erin's remark suggests, changes in my basic mood were not altogether problematic. Several friends joked about my having found nirvana on the fast-track—I seemed all zen, all the time. There were, however, rare times when my changed wiring led me to tears, usually in response to a question about what I wanted. For example, well into a searching phone call, a close friend said, "You're sounding tired. Do you want me to get off the phone and leave you alone now?"

I repeated aloud, "Do I want…?" and did a quick self-check. There I was once again, listening in to my own mind, awaiting a reply and getting none—no expression of desire or will. And yet the question implied that I should or might want something.

"I don't know," I said. Tears spilled down my face. "I don't know how to answer the question." For a moment, I grieved the emptiness in my head, paradoxically saddened by my own lack of emotion. But then the winds changed, the inner clouds moved again and my access to this light-shaft of sensation disappeared.

Generally, I was more curious than upset about my condition. When another friend asked a version of the inevitable "Are you angry?" question, I pointed out that the same whack on the head that messed with my frontal lobes' administrative abilities had also muted my affect so I could not despair.

"Lucky," I said.

"That's not luck," he said, "that's grace. That's the universe making sure you can handle what it's given you."

*　*　*　*

Perhaps the universe should have known better than to allow me to put that offer down on the Fort Langley apartment. Mid-January, we moved from our many-roomed home on a large lot to a tiny two-bedroom apartment. And then the last, most dramatic change struck: depression. It struck so hard and fast that it seems to me now as if I went to sleep one night a not-unhappy-soul and woke up inside a cloud of grief. Really, the onset was slightly less dramatic, taking about two weeks.

Depression is so common with head injuries that a doctor at the Early Intervention Brain Injury Clinic predicted upon first meeting me that it lay in my path. I hadn't exactly scoffed at his remark, but given my blissed-out mood then, I couldn't imagine my psyche taking such a turn. I have no journal record of my early descent into the dark (because I'd packed my health journal in one of forty-five identical boxes), but in my first entry from the apartment, February 2005, I note, *I've begun to feel down in a way I haven't all fall. The bliss or mellowness is dissipating....*

This was no fleeting mood swing. After the whirlwind of preparations and a major move, I hit a wall and stopped functioning.

How to account for depression? Having lived with family members afflicted with both manic-depressive and depressive illness, I appreciate the difference between temporary sadness due to life circumstances—death, divorce—and the sort of unprovoked crash of someone suffering unhappy brain chemistry. Over the decade prior to 2004, I had found myself occasionally slipping into one or two week long "blue" periods, characterized by pervasive sadness, a sense that, despite demonstrable reasons for happiness in my life—chiefly Erin and Tillie, my good health, my dear friends—I lacked access to some essential source of meaning, of joy. These moods tended to descend when my hands were idle, at the close of a big project or end of a busy season. I learned to pick myself up psychologically by "picking myself up" physically, becoming active. Gardening and landscaping were favourite therapeutics. But really, I would busy my hands with anything if I could thereby outrun my mind. (Once, I'd spent a Friday night sorting the contents of a small mechanic's cabinet with eighteen tiny drawers full of nails, screws, batteries. I not only sorted nails from screws, I cleaned each one before stashing them away again. I really would do *anything* to keep from idleness.)

Not long before the Maritime vacation, I'd visited a naturopath, my much-deferred fortieth birthday present to myself. I went for what I thought of as a midlife tune-up. My only health complaints were an arthritic knee and episodic insomnia, yet I found myself telling the doctor of a recent ennui, my inclination to withdraw socially, avoid answering the phone, decline contact with friends, all of which I'd begun noticing. She suggested I might be mildly depressed and prescribed St. John's wort, which I'd been taking since. I noted in my health journal that the herb seemed to buoy me up. But by the time we moved, it was no longer enough.

And then I went back to work.

At the College, my department Chair had arranged as low-stress a teaching load as possible for me: two combined sections of a single course, no back-to-back classes or late nights. But the complex cognitive effort involved in academic work did me in. I slept eight to ten hours every night, yet found myself fighting sleep in the car on the drive home, and falling into a foggy-headed stupor as soon as I reached the couch, no matter how early my day ended. And all this was prior to the move in mid-January. Afterwards, I relapsed completely. There were too many decisions to make at the new place—and they were too interdependent for me to know how to begin—so I made none. I took to wandering zombie-like around the apartment, avoiding towers of unpacked boxes and side-stepping unhung pictures. I slept without sheets on my bed for three weeks, partly because I couldn't think my way through unearthing the linen, partly because my room was so crammed with up-ended furniture and more boxes that I preferred not to enter it until I had to, for sleep. When the shelf in my bedroom closet crashed to the floor, I walked away from the disaster. A day or two later, I tried briefly to muster the ability to think through how to re-mount the brackets. But I failed, so I left the collapsed shelf, and all the previously-ironed work clothes, now crushed and buried, for another two weeks. It didn't help that every time I left the bedroom, I'd forget about the chaos of the closet. Each rediscovery led me to say, "Oh, I forgot. This fell down." Again and again, new information. I washed and re-wore the same two teaching outfits for three weeks.

In the classroom, my cognitive deficits led to situations that would have embarrassed or distressed me if I'd had the capacity to be embarrassed or distressed. On teaching mornings, I woke with no idea what my subject was to be that day: I'd glance at my syllabus over breakfast (ah, comparison/contrast essays…), only to forget again by the time I'd driven to work. Luckily, I was teaching a course I'd taught many times and could reach into my filing cabinet for lecture notes and hand-outs to be adapted each week. In class, my memory gaps must have been apparent to students: once, I dismissed class only to be approached by a timid, perplexed young man, concerned that I'd begun lecture by announcing that we'd cover three topics that day and then had covered only two. (*Huh?*, I thought.) Another day, I handed back marked assignments and wished the students a fine weekend, only to notice two puzzled young men peering at their syllabus, struggling with the ethical question of whether to remind me they were supposed to write a test that day, or just run off. Several times I walked into class clutching hand-outs, only to find them still in my clutches after everyone had gone. At my counselor's urging, I took to writing myself notes and lists before class, but that effort ended with me pulling the list out of my briefcase only once I was back in my office, *after* class. Reminder notes can't help if you don't remember writing them.

My headaches escalated to the point that I became preoccupied with recording their triggers, frequency and duration. But my journal entries are full of doubts and questions: did you take that pill or not? I was interested especially in tracking the effectiveness of Toradol, a prescription analgesic. Unfortunately, by the time I'd sit to record symptoms at the end of each day, I'd often forgotten the details. The entries become ragged, as if thinking in whole sentences were too taxing, as in this entry from mid-February: *10 pm, crashing headache, and numb/dumb. Maybe I took a 3rd Toradol? Don't recall—if so, it's just worn off. Acute headache. Sleep now.*

And then sadness descended. In an early February entry I wrote, *Last night I thought about suicide for the first time in a long time.... Under perpetual head-fog, headache, fatigue and sense of incredible limitation to what I can do. I'm mostly too tired to want to try, or too unfocussed to remember that I need to try—should want to try. And I'm feeling acutely alone. Lonely.*

Sliding swiftly into grief, a week later I wrote, *very sad. Don't care. Headache back..., but maybe 'cause I'm thinking. Just so damned sad.* The next day: *church on Sunday: weepy over Valentine's day.* The next: *Felt very down again in evening.*

Depression is a bleak, lonely place. I suffered many usual symptoms: lack of initiative, distorted perceptions, withdrawal from friends and family. Other symptoms, such as profound fatigue and loss of concentration, had been part of my head injury experience all fall anyway, and of course persisted. I began to break engagements and avoid telephone calls. I felt an overwhelming desire to fade from other people's view. As many depressives do, I felt I stood apart, separate from others who could not possibly understand my world, coloured in its distorting hue of unremitting grief. I spent all my undirected time with tears in my eyes— sometimes a subdued, quiet crying, others a loud wailing.

And yet I functioned at work, if minimally. I could instruct students in the shape of a well-developed academic paragraph, greet colleagues in the hallways. All the time, I harboured the solipsistic conviction that other people's lives were somehow not real. The classroom seemed an artificial environment; looking out from the podium was like looking at fish through glass at the aquarium. I watched students file out of lecture, thinking, "You have no idea what I'm going through." I'd be weeping before I reached the parkade. It seems to me I wept for weeks, crying simply because I was awake. My grief was free-floating, too, yet liable to latch on to any excuse. Looking at a mug, I'd recall the year the Easter Bunny packed it into Erin's basket, and I'd cry over the cruelty of time. The sight of an empty swing at a playground led to instant regret that I hadn't gone often enough to the park when the girls were small, hadn't pushed them high enough, hadn't shared their dizzying thrill at being young and pumping high over the tree tops. Despair weighted me down, a lead stone in my stomach. I feared the girls would outgrow me soon, leave their childhoods behind without enough happy memories of quality time with Mum. I'd wasted my life, I'd done it all wrong. More tears.

Other triggers, perhaps more reasonable causes for sadness, arose from my distant past. I hurt afresh over having been abandoned by my mother when I was five, again when I was fourteen, by my father when I was five, again when I was eight, finally by his death when I was eighteen. Nor could I stop myself from dwelling on more recent sorrows: one of my sisters, mentally ill, has become one of Vancouver's "lost" homeless; her ex-husband, who'd been in my teenaged years a surrogate uncle/father, killed himself the same week in 1998 that I'd discovered my husband was having an affair. My closest friend was currently drifting away from me into alcoholism. These sorrows vied for my attention as I sat among heaps of unopened boxes. I noted in my journal, *am quite aware...how easily I can be caught in the weepies or sense of despair. I've thought to myself I feel as if I'm on the verge of crying for all the years of grief, and all the losses. I do think it possible that once I started, I would never stop. Never.*

The Sunday afternoon before Valentine's Day, I simply failed to rise to my parenting role. I'd told the girls we'd go down to the village shops to buy gifts for the special boy in each of their lives. But I couldn't stop crying long enough to get out the door. I sat at the kitchen table all afternoon, periodically drying my eyes, saying "Soon." While I sat, the "solution" of taking pills crossed my mind. I had lots of pills. Toradol. Alertec. Sleeping pills. I wasn't so far along in ideation as to be designing a particular cocktail, but I was aware of the flickering image of release, registering the siren-like promise of any kind of end to sadness. Yet such moments only spurred me on to more grief, more tears for the immediate guilt at imagining I might abandon my lovely daughters. I wrestled with the desire to stay alive to their emotional realities, beating myself up at being so selfish as to consider depriving them of the unconditional love parents owe their children, inflicting on them the very abandonment that had begun my own sadness in childhood. But it wasn't a battle I was sure I could win.

To the outer eye, I probably looked comatose, except for the tears; inside, my mind swung like a farm gate on a stormy night—crashing open, smashing shut— as I grieved chaotically, pulled between the medicine cabinet, with its anaesthetic promise, and my shame at harbouring such traitorous thoughts. Eventually, locked at the table in this invisible battle, I told the girls to take my wallet and go shopping on their own. I couldn't go with them this time. They agreed, and as they readied themselves in the hallway, perversely, I began crying even harder—now devastated by their apparent ability to carry on without me, even though I'd asked them to do so.

Then, from behind, I felt the small, soft hand of my eleven-year-old baby, Tillie. She lifted my head out of my hands, wrapped her arms around my shoulders and laid her cool cheek against mine, clinging to me silently for a long minute while I tried to quell the coming sobs.

Hanging on so tight that I couldn't lean back to look her in the face, she said quietly, "I need you, Mummy."

I gasped at her intuitive grasp of the dangerous place I'd gone inside.

"What made you say that?"

She shook her head. "I don't know. But I do." And she held on for another long minute before joining her sister. Then they were off, in search of candies for their sweethearts. A short while later, they returned with their gifts—and a bouquet of daisies for me. Big Marguerites, they told me. Sunny blossoms named after me.

First thing Monday morning, I phoned a nurse on the brain injury team. Ever the mistress of understatement, I said, "I don't seem to be coping well." She arranged a clinic session in a few days. I made it through those last bleak hours believing relief was near. I credit the intuitive touch of a heart-full daughter. Or maybe I'm alive simply because there was sunshine one dark day, instead of rain. Who knows why one pulls through?

Luckily, my depression was responsive to medication. I found my balance again. With the help of daily pills and regular therapy, I explored and accepted what it means to live inside a changed brain. Despite medical prognoses that further recovery after two years is unlikely, or insignificant, I continued to "come back" to myself well into the third year, post trauma. And as of this writing, I am again alive to insight—or it to me—working happily in the ever-surprising realms of symbol, intuition and dream.

A Long Day's Journey into...

The story of Ashley as told to her friend, Karen Kristjanson

Ashley was living her life full-force. When describing her life before the accident last March she tells me "I was doing everything! Working fifteen-hour days, running, traveling, being totally social." At the age of twenty-six, Ashley had earned her chartered accountancy designation and soon after found her dream job with a large consulting firm. With her high energy and active lifestyle, she counted multi-tasking as one of her most precious strengths.

And then, ten months ago, Ashley's life hit a wall.

Strictly speaking, it wasn't a wall. One Thursday afternoon in March 2013, Ashley was in the passenger seat of a friend's Honda that was rear-ended while waiting at a red light. After the initial *wham* Ashley and her friend clambered out of the car, shaken. Ashley remembers the other driver, a large thirty-something man, first commenting, "No need to call the police, is there?" This struck her as kind of shady. "Then he attempted to minimize the collision, saying, 'At least it wasn't that hard!'" and I just said, 'You're kidding, that was really hard!'"

After exchanging vehicle information, the two friends kept driving, shocked and unsure of what to do next. Ashley's neck and back hurt a lot and she was feeling nauseous. She knew this was a bad sign. Finally, her friend pulled the car over and Ashley remained in her seat, staring ahead blankly. "I felt surreal - disconnected from everything around me. We got out of the car and wandered around for a few minutes and finally we sat down on a rock." Ashley's cell phone rang - it was her mother. Ashley had called her, hung up when her mother answered and had instantly forgotten that she had phoned. Her mother urged Ashley to go to an emergency room hospital.

The next few days remain muddled in Ashley's memory. By the time she reached the ER, she was feeling extremely nauseous. The doctor on call paid scant attention to her symptoms. After a cursory examination lasting perhaps six minutes, he concluded that Ashley had mild post-concussion symptoms. He told her to take a couple of days off work and to call him if things got worse. Although Ashley had little confidence in the doctor's assessment, she complied, staying home for two days. Her pain and nausea intensified. On the third day, she got dressed and went into work. She made it into the office, but had significant pain, and couldn't focus her eyes. When she tried to read, she felt sick. Then her nose started to bleed. Her supervisor took one look at her and said, "You look terrible. Go home."

Ironically this wasn't Ashley's first experience with these kinds of symptoms. During her third year of university, she had been hit hard in a rugby scrum, knocked unconscious and trampled for a few seconds. She had no memory of the first hours that followed but knew that her doctor had told her to take the accident seriously, recommending that Ashley give up dodge ball, kickboxing, snowboarding. He warned her that a second concussion could be really serious. The five weeks that followed that accident had been lost in terms of Ashley's university studies as she hadn't been able to read without getting nauseated. However, the symptoms slowly abated and she managed to complete her academic year. The experience left Ashley with an acute awareness of her brain and what it meant in her life. And reluctantly, she did stop all high-impact activities.

So this, her second concussion, was deeply frightening. When Ashley left work that day she went straight to the walk-in clinic. By the time she arrived she was dry-heaving – her body wanting to vomit but with nothing there to expel. This time a different doctor checked her more thoroughly and said, "You need to lie down for a week. Then try short walks, start at five minutes a day and work up to ten minutes. Gentle walks. Add more walking gradually and check back with me in three weeks. No work for at least a month."

Ashley slowly walked out of his office, overwhelmed. "I sat down and sobbed. I didn't even know how to get home – they told me I shouldn't have even walked to the clinic. I was appalled at his verdict. This was so not what I wanted to hear!" She was utterly miserable. "My head hurt, my back hurt, my neck hurt, I felt sick, I couldn't focus on anything." Realizing how incapacitated she was, Ashley's roommate took her to her mother's house, where she slept eighteen hours a day for the first week. The former high-achiever had no appetite, couldn't read, couldn't even look at a TV or computer screen. She felt totally exhausted. "Occasionally I would feel a bit better, strong enough to sit up and look outside at the yard. That was my highlight of the day!"

The second week brought some slight improvement. When talking with friends, Ashley would try to report any accomplishments. One time she was proud to share her biggest achievement of the day, "I downloaded a podcast today." What she didn't share was that she had lacked the energy to listen to it and had had to wait for the next day when she listened for five minutes and then stopped, drained by the effort of focusing. "I felt totally unhappy and frustrated. My mom got the brunt of my misery. I felt so helpless and dependent I couldn't even complete the forms that Employment Insurance sent me!" These forms came by email, and she couldn't read them, much less fill them out. Her mother read them out aloud to her and recorded Ashley's answers on the sheets.

One of the aspects that terrified Ashley the most was the unknown. Although her neurologist had reassured her that most concussion patients fully recover within one year or two, Ashley wondered if her brain would ever regain its former condition. She knew that in a very real way our brains make us who we are and the looming question of what her recovered self would be was always with her.

Progress meant Ashley was able to take three minute walks which she, oh-so-gradually, extended over the next three weeks. At this point she moved back to her own apartment with her roommate for support. Sleep was her only method of pain management, so she took naps many times each day. Regular stimulus was an overwhelming assault to her senses: music, someone clicking their pen while talking to her, the blare of traffic sounds, hearing multiple conversations swirling around her in a coffee shop. She couldn't tolerate having many people around, bright lights, music of any sort, so her roommate kept their apartment quiet and dim for months.

Going back to work at this point was clearly impossible. At the follow-up appointment her doctor told her there was no way she should consider returning to work for at least another month. Ashley hated the news but being given a longer timeline was helpful. "I couldn't see any progress from day-to-day. So not having to hold myself under a microscope each day was good for me. Looking on a weekly basis, I could see small improvements." It helped too, that her doctor gave her a list of things she could be doing. He explained that the medical understanding of concussions was evolving, urging her to be active at small levels and to push herself but not too far. For the formerly active young woman it was a relief to finally have some things she could actually do.

Ashley enrolled in an occupational therapy (OT) post-concussion program in June. The first assessment lasted three hours and the effort of concentrating on various diagnostic questions brought her to exhausted tears. From that point on though, she found the program a terrific support, providing her with a plan of action that challenged both her brain and her body. The OT therapist was a shoulder for Ashley to lean on. "It was so nice to have her. It got so tiring having to explain everything at each appointment to someone new – I couldn't trust myself to remember all the important things. Once I was in the program, this therapist knew me and my experience."

Also in June, desperate to maintain some professional connection, Ashley tried returning to work for one hour each day. It was far too soon. "Just getting showered and into a suit, walking to work – that exhausted me before I even arrived. When I did, people were inquiring about me and how I was doing. It was too much to handle." She left quickly, feeling frustrated and inadequate.

The contrast between her healthy-looking exterior and the reality of her struggling interior was both wearying and isolating. "This is an invisible condition which makes it so much harder. People look at me and they see a young, fit person and there are no cues unless I explain. And even then they may not get it. They say 'You look great!' and it's like a punch in the gut, because how I look has nothing to do with what I'm struggling with...People can't understand. If you can get through the basics of living, people assign you the full range of abilities." Even more difficult was that other people's expectations often led to periods of self-doubt, requiring Ashley to review her own reality to make sure it was still that bad. "I felt down and anxious so much."

Ashley's condition tested all of her social relationships. She felt wonderfully supported by her family but friends sorted themselves by their actions and some didn't follow through. "They would ask, 'What can I do to help?' and I would say 'Well, I can do quiet tea dates and forty-five minute walks.' 'Great,' they would say, 'let me know when you're up for that.' I would explain 'Well, I'm always free now, YOU let ME know.' And I would never hear from them. I learned that their promises were completely empty." But other friends were wonderful and were there for her again and again. "I valued so much their support and understanding. My relationship with my boyfriend was tough. He's far away, he couldn't do that much and partners do want to fix you...It didn't help that the condition made me so irritable a lot of the time. I remember snapping at him, 'How do you think my day was!'" But having survived such a test strengthened their connection. "This probably won't be the hardest thing that will happen to me or to us. It's reassuring to know he's the kind of guy who would see me through this."

As she strengthened, Ashley began making small steps towards returning to work. She volunteered for a non-profit organization, editing a paper and speeches at her own pace at home. This helped her build up stamina for looking at a computer screen. "It gave me a sense of accomplishment – I so needed that!" In September Ashley began working for her firm from home, one hour at a time. She started working in a quiet spot in her apartment, then shifted to a reading room in a nearby community centre, and then to a quiet coffee shop. At the same time, she increased the frequency of her work periods and then the duration. The steps helped her to improve her ability to stay focused when working near activities and distractions until she was ready to return to her workplace.

Today, almost a year post-concussion, Ashley has made huge progress. She is back at her firm, putting in eighteen-hour days of demanding work. This is what is expected of professionals at her level and she is not only willing to do it but grateful that she can. At the same time, she monitors herself carefully, knowing that occasionally she can still hit the limit of her own capacities. Not wanting to be seen as less than fully capable by her employers, she keeps these struggles to herself and carries on as best as she can. Socially there continue to be challenges too. Sometimes she'll be at a restaurant and suddenly the music and crush of people become too much and she has to leave. Compared to a year ago, Ashley looks normal yet she is like a colour photograph that is almost but not yet fully developed. The bright colours are there but their depth and intensity are slightly muted.

Not surprisingly, the events of the past year have changed Ashley. While she has always been very socially aware, most of her life experience was one of health and independence. Now she knows what it is like to live with chronic pain and to be dependent on those around her. "A friend of mine injured her shoulder recently and I was really aware that she couldn't carry her bags herself but didn't want to ask for help – something I wouldn't have been conscious of before the accident." Her compassion has entirely new dimensions. Ashley now has a profound appreciation – almost reverence – for her brain. "What I take away from this is that my brain still works. I'll be fine. We need our brains to work – without that, nothing is good. The terror of not knowing if my brain would ever recover was overwhelming."

Now Ashley's doctors tell her that she's doing great and that it's still early days for a post-concussion syndrome. They reassure her that although healthcare professionals don't know exactly how concussion impacts the brain's functioning, they do know that time and patience will usually restore the brain to its former self. Ashley is traveling on a journey to an unknown destination. Her message to others is, "Never say to someone with a concussion, 'At least you're alive, at least you can still walk,' and try to find a silver lining. Until you know your brain is okay, there is no silver lining! Say 'This is brutal. I'm glad you are talking about it with me.'

A Raspberry Torte

Myna Wallin

I heard about the accident and what had really happened much later on. My sister and her friend were just leaving the studio where they'd spent the morning drawing. They were chatting, discussing where on Queen among the trendy restaurants they'd go for lunch, when my sister went splat, slipping on a patch of ice. Not realizing the degree of the injury and that in fact she had sustained a dangerous blow to her head, my sister quickly tried to get up. When she couldn't, she told her friend to "let me rest here a while, I'll be fine." Like a drunk who passes out on a sidewalk grate, or someone in a snowdrift suffering from frostbite, she just wanted to have a "little nap," and that seemed reasonable to her, in that moment. Just a little shut-eye, while her skull bled onto the ice beneath her. Her friend Beth, convinced my sister that perhaps she should get up and have it checked out, to be on the "safe side." It took a lot of coercion because of course she was perfectly "fine". Everyone in my family is always "fine". I remember my father telling my mother to "Go back to sleep, you'll be fine in the morning," when she was undergoing chemotherapy. (She came to my room instead, but that's another story.)

❧ ❧ ❧ ❧

"She's confused, doesn't know her own phone number. Yours was in her phone." It was my sister's artist friend calling me from the studio they shared on Tecumseh. A long pause came next, as though the words were not only too difficult to speak but too difficult to arrange in any coherent-sounding way. "Can you come to the hospital, your sister slipped ... there was ice ... a lot of blood … but she'll be okay. I don't mean to scare you..." While Beth rambled on about my sister's accident, I sat in my apartment, a piece of half-chewed bagel in my mouth. I wasn't sure why I was the one getting the emergency call, my sister was married. Then Beth reminded me - my brother-in-law was in Calgary on business.

❧ ❧ ❧ ❧

I arrived at the hospital within minutes, screaming at the taxi driver the whole way to hurry the hell up. This was an unusual situation in so many ways. It was usually -- no always -- me who was the one in distress. A history of depression, and being the unmarried sister, left me vulnerable, needing her help. Not the other way around. My sister didn't look like herself. First of all, there was a cloud of confusion wrapped around her. "Are you okay? Are you in pain?" I sat down beside her on the cot in the emergency room. "I got blood on my new coat. I don't think it'll come out." She was rubbing at her new green parka with her free hand and a piece of paper towel. "Let me see your head, can you lift up the gauze for a second?"

She held up a clump of reddened bandage on her head, the hair all around it was matted and wet with blood. A flap of skin exposed what looked like the mushy centre of a raspberry torte. The site of the wound seemed to spread over half her skull. I felt queasy. I wanted to scream, "Where is your nurse, have they given you a pain killer, what is going on here!" But I knew it was my job to remain calm and relatively in control. I didn't want to scare her. I learned hospital protocol a long, long time ago. "It's nothing," my sister said, "I've got to go home and get dinner ready for the kids."

Meantime, the deep red raspberry blood was dripping onto her hand and down her neck to her sweater. She was badly hurt and didn't seem to realize it. I was terrified. The nurse poked her head in, behind the curtain to ask if we needed anything. The doctor would be with us shortly. "Some fresh gauze, please," I nearly shouted. "And some water."

"Oh, you can help yourself to water down the hall," she answered, blithely ignoring the urgency in my voice. This was the Emergency Department. Everybody's injuries were an emergency. You waited in line according to the life threat of your injury: broken limbs, hearts refusing to pump. God knows what else. I heard police rumbling around the back, there was probably a gunshot victim that got precedence.

My sister told me she had slipped on a patch of ice in front of her studio. She wasn't sure how it happened. It was the landlord's job, he was supposed to clear the ice and snow in front of the building they were renting. She had just had a really good session with a favourite model and was happy with her drawing. Why was everyone "making such a fuss." It was just a bump. She needed to pick up food for the kids, prepare dinner and take a nap. She'd be fine. She just had a bad headache and felt a bit sleepy. "You should probably get that looked at, since you're here," I said. "Here, let me see if I can get the blood off your jacket."

The doctor sewed her up right in front of me. I was sure I'd never get the opportunity to see a head wound this close again. I was fascinated. What amazed me was that the gash was not neat and tidy, with clean edges. When the doctor lifted the flaps of skin to sew up her scalp on the left side of her head, it was a mess. He had to fold the skin twice over to keep it from leaving a hole. Some of the skin must have ripped off and stuck to the ice.

"I don't need stitches, I'm sure it's nothing," my sister kept insisting. She didn't like needles of any kind.

"Just a couple, hold still please." She ended up with twelve stitches. It was definitely something.

I peered so close to the sewing, the doctor asked me back up. "You're in my light," he said, and then shooed me away. "That's enough, I've got to close up."

The nurse left me with instructions for cleaning the wound and so forth. Most importantly, I was to wake my sister up every hour during the night and ask her something innocuous like her middle name, or what day it was, or what her address was. This was because her state of confusion during and after her fall was worrisome. My sister later admitted that she was upset by it, too.

"I wonder why I couldn't remember my phone number. Probably because I was so pissed off at our landlord."

I slept over at my sister's that night for the first time since our father had died and I came back from England for the funeral. It was the first time I'd slept in her bed since we were kids. No point sleeping across the hall. I had to make sure she didn't stop breathing.

I don't know if my sister knows this to this day or if she realizes the effect it had on me. But I didn't sleep that night. I watched her sleep and listened to her, making sure she was breathing. If she stopped breathing it would be my responsibility.

So I woke her every hour. "What's the address of your house?" and "Who is the Prime Minister?" and "How old are you?" and so on. Sometimes I asked her two or three questions before I let her go back to sleep. She swatted the questions away like flies and made it through the night with flying colours.

Months later, over the phone, my sister said, "I just don't understand why I am still getting these headaches. It's crazy. I slipped and fell ages ago."

"Well you had a concussion. It was serious. You had stitches. I was there, remember?"

"No. It was nothing. They said it might have been a concussion. I had a couple of stitches. It wasn't serious. You exaggerate everything, Myna."

"Well, it's a head wound and it takes time to heal. Take a Tylenol if you need one. Don't be a martyr."

"I'm fine," she said, and then said good night, she had to tuck the kids into bed.

LIVING THE DREAM

Heather Williams

In 2001 I was living my dream dancing and singing at Universal Studio Japan. Apparently on the evening of July 14th I chose to leave a Karaoke bar earlier than others, hopped on my bike and left alone. I was hit by a taxi. Ambulance personnel chose to take me to Dr. Wakai, a specialist in head injuries at Osaka National Hospital.

On Vancouver Island, Canada, at noon July 13th, my mom and sister Emily struggled to translate a message from Japan. They had the phone company help. Then "Moshi, Moshi, Ah Mamasan, Heathesan coma. Then "Y'al don't know me. I'm Hillary, a friend of Heather's. She's been hit by a taxi and never regained consciousness. Betta c'm quick".

The urgency to cross half the world propelled them into action. The travel agent asked, "You've got current passport eh?" Mom didn't! Canadian Foreign Affairs needed to create a special passport. They were up all night notifying pertinent people, especially my boyfriend, booking off work, arranging house/animal care and financial assistance. They caught the 5:15 a.m. ferry to Vancouver to join sister Sarah. Both sisters had passports and vied for mom's ticket. Sarah went, she was a nursing student. Emily and Mom bought two tickets for a flight 24 hours later.

The phone call. Sarah had seen me and through an interpreter had some questions answered, "She's a lefty, Mom, and paralyzed down the left side. Please get here" Late on Monday evening, Mom and Emily crept quietly to ICU, Osaka National Hospital. The nurses and Dr. Wakai bowed saying, "Konichiwa", Hello. Em rushed to my side, kissed me and talked into my ear. Mom held my hand and wept. They were taken to KKR Hotel Osaka and went to bed exhausted.

Doctor Wakai had limited English. "Grim" was the word to describe my MRI results. They predict I will not resume consciousness for two to three weeks and cannot say what brain damage may have occurred. When leaving a nurse handed them my laundry and through charades conveyed they were responsible for it.

The next day Mom notes they were cranky and snapping at each other. They hated waking up to this horrible reality.

As days passed a routine developed, laundry, emailing, discovering Osaka, and visiting me on the allotted times. They distracted themselves making origami cranes and socializing with my cast and the arrival of my boyfriend

Sarah had to return to her nursing course in Canada.

6 weeks post accident - Excerpt from Emily's email;

"As of yesterday our little Heddy was kicking up a storm so the nurses decided to make a Japanese style bed and put her on the floor. It rocks! They padded the walls with huge pieces of cardboard. It is basically a king size bed X2 to roll around on. Now she is freer but this makes it very difficult to feed and suction her."

For meals I sat in a wheelchair with an Obi around my torso. My meals were presented to me in true Japanese fashion. A member of the kitchen staff would bow and let me smell it, then feed me through my nasal gastric tube.

I started to receive physiotherapy and he used the Bobath method..

Mom contacted the Canadian Consulate to ask for help in repatriating and transporting me to Canada. "Patient Link," a Canadian patient transport was discovered.

They secured 9 seats on the direct, Air Canada commercial flight for a stretcher, the nurse, Mom and Emily.

BC Ambulance transported me to the Neurological Ward of Vancouver General Hospital. Apparently I hugged my friends with my right arm but I don't remember this! Various professionals arrived. The dietitian requested a canned formula running 24/7 through a feeding tube. In Japan I had three squares a day, which worked perfectly. They didn't want to hear about Japan. The doctor wondered aloud, why I didn't have burr holes in my cranium? The psych resident ordered a chemical restraint. Mom was extremely exasperated, "Have you even read her Japanese chart, which had been translated into English? It's 9 weeks post accident!" It was a different philosophy to what they experienced in Japan.

September 8th I evidently pulled out my trach, calmly placed it on my chest and continued to breathe on my own.

I was so doped up on nozinan that I was unable to participate in the G. F. Strong Rehabilitation Centre assessment. They stated I wouldn't be eligible for at least 6 weeks. September 11, 2001 a wave of terror in America. Thursday, September 13th moving day! Apparently mom found me sitting in a wheelchair peering through my flowers. The nurse stated, "She's being transferred to G. F. Strong right now. We need her bed in case there is an attack on the west coast." As they hooked my wheelchair by chains into the Handi-Dart, there was a cranking sound.

(THIS IS MY FIRST MEMORY SINCE MY ACCIDENT)!

My memory then started to return in flashes. Lifting out of my coma was like waking up from an anesthetic.

I was then taken to the Acquired Brain Injury ward. The therapy teams began assessing me and were somewhat alarmed at my premature admission.

My daily therapies were physio, speech, occupational therapy, and frequent naps. I was not aware enough to tell time or able to wheel myself to therapies so family members or friends were needed. I was keen about physio because I was determined to walk. Physical work was familiar to me. I ripped my nasal gastric tube out exclaiming, "Out. My nose hurts. I'm sorry." I had to eat enough so it wouldn't be reinserted.

On the journey to speech therapy Mom prompted me with the day, the time, and my meal. When quizzed I got it all wrong! According to me, it was night on Sunday and apparently I hadn't had a meal.

My physiotherapist suggested a walker. I sat there with a sullen look on my face. He then suggested a fire engine red walker. I shook my head stating "for old people." A compromise was pushing my wheelchair.

We took the ferry for my first trip home in 9 months. I was slumped over in my wheelchair when the bell for the announcements came on. I perked up very aware. "I remember the bing-bong" and began to cry. On return to G. F. Strong my boyfriend had arrived for a short visit. We were offered a friend's condo. If I came to my therapies 5 days a week the team thought it would be a good experience. It was very cozy and easy for my friends to come and visit.

October 25th team meeting.

The notes state;

Heather was injured in Japan on July 14, 2001.

Her Glasgow Coma was reported to be 7 at the scene, with decerebrate posturing.

She sustained the following injuries;

Severe head injury

Left clavicle fracture

Fractured base of skull

Facial injury to the left frontal region

Since Heather's admission to G. F. Strong she has made a number of physical, as well as cognitive gains. She no longer requires the use of medications for agitation. No longer requires a NG tube. She continues to have some evidence of impulsivity but this is improving. Her speech is somewhat slow but improved in clarity. Increasing range has been noted in the left arm. Cognitively she continues to have word finding difficulty and memory problems. I have referred her to neuro-opthalmology regarding vision.

My new O.T. started me on the computer and I acquired an e-mail address. When cooking we would end up in stitches because I was a lefty.

Friends organized a dinner for my 24th birthday, December 1st. A year before I had celebrated my birthday with my boyfriend in Hong Kong. This year he came to stay at the condo with us for three days. He treated me like a fragile doll. I was aware enough to know he was physically and emotionally pulling away. Before he left he got a queasy stomach, which was telling.

MY DISCHARGE FROM G. F. Strong was December 18th, 2001.

Heather Williams is a 24-year-old female who suffered a severe head injury on July 14th, 2001. She continues to present with difficulties in abstract thought, judgment and simple arithmetic. Her speech is slow. She continues to have left-sided weakness both in the upper and lower extremity with bilateral ataxia.

The subsequent follow-up was organized:

1. Doctor of physical medicine/rehabilitation

2. Doctor of orthopedics for removal of clavicle pin

3. Neuro-opthalmology regarding vision

4. Neuropsychology to establish a base line for cognitive functioning

5. Speech therapy

6. Physio and occupational therapy

7. Sexual health G. F. Strong team available if needed

8. ABI education: Risk of seizures with injuries such as mine. Safety issues – fire, alcohol, protective headwear, avoid diving and I was unable to drive.

9. Her mood should be monitored over the next months for any sign of increasing frustration or sadness, which may emerge as she gains awareness of her situation.

Then she tried to explain what had happened to me and drew a picture of the brain. I had a severe closed head injury. There was evidence both on CT scans and MRI of the brain, which shows intraventricular hemorrhage of the right thalamic splenium, right temporal cortex, left frontal corpus callasum and left frontal subcortex contusion. I also suffered a base skull fracture. Multiple facial fractures particularly in the right frontal region. The primary injury was a diffuse axonal injury. The stretching and tearing of the fine threadlike nerve cells throughout the brain altered the function of the cells and their ability to communicate with each other. Although I didn't understand all of this and the medical terms were like Greek.

(In hindsight I would have gained more if the medical personnel reviewed this summary frequently).

Mom bought a wheelchair and we headed home to stay. Thankfully our home was all on one level. Soon the walls acquired handprints from my wall walking.

I felt speech and physiotherapy at Nanaimo Regional General Hospital were futile. I was put on a treadmill at NRGH and left alone. No one was there to remind me of proper gait. I wanted "Heather therapy", dancing, singing and playing piano. I visited a neuropsychologist. I remember listening to her findings with great clarity. She stated, "Heather is on the left side of the bell curve. It is unlikely she will be able to learn anything new or multitask. There are significant problems with vision functioning." I sat slumped over in my wheelchair feeling defeated. I cried all the way home. Mom was at a loss for words. All I knew was that I was going to prove the findings wrong.

I was slowly waking up and feeling restless. I wanted to go. Where? My boyfriend was in L.A. with his band. Emily said she would accompany me for a week. He was tentative with me and the man who expressed his undying love was not there. I felt like damaged goods. I cried all the way home.

I reconnected with a high school friend. I offered to pay all the time for her acceptance. She had a car and I couldn't drive any longer. This gave me a sense of freedom. She dreamed of going to Mexico. I wanted to keep on running so we took a trip to Puerto Vallarta. My family was horrified. I would be spending the money I saved in Japan and missing therapies. I didn't care because I was disillusioned with therapy. No one could stop my impulsivity.

As we entered the plane a flight attendant made a gesture with her hand mimicking drinking. My friend explained I was injured.

On arrival we met 5 Mexican men. One spoke English quite well. There was some conversation and flirting. We piled into the back of their pick up and drove around Puerto Vallarta drinking beer.

July 14, 2002 – Mom's journal

Recently Heather has scared me when she fell twice. She refuses to use her wheelchair anymore. This stubborn independence is good for rehab but risky at times. She also went through a period of stating she "should have died in the accident". She dislikes people telling her she should be so glad to be alive. She yearns for a better quality of life. The trips she has taken with a companion to assist her are her attempts at distraction and fulfilling the time it will take to recover. The family continues to deal with the overwhelming reality of what has happened. Some days it is tough!

I lived in Vancouver with a friend and went twice a day for 3 weeks to the hyperbaric oxygen chamber. I know it made some difference but it wasn't the miracle cure I hoped it would be.

My trip to Mexico motivated me to take Spanish lessons. I reached an intermediate level. Ha, I could learn something new. During this time I reconnected with a dancing friend and did baby ballet with her.

Excerpt - Mom's journal December 2002;

Woke this a.m. and finally tapped into my sorrow and grief re: Heddy's accident. Right now I am struggling with advocating and supporting her while she tries to get her life back. Last eve we went to a movie and while waiting for the taxi she told me she feels she has a black cloud hanging over her. It has been so long and she is so unhappy. She often states she wishes she had died. I do as well sometimes. This is Hell! She was gifted, beautiful, and full of potential. She went to Japan and succeeded. Now she is beautiful but disabled. Canada has agreed she's disabled and she has a small pension. Not enough to survive. The money she saved in Japan is gone and she worries about tomorrow, so do I. Her sisters are not around. They are affected but now seem so impatient and critical with her. Perhaps they're own feelings of loss cause this. The lawyer questions fault and this concerned me re: settlement. She has had her life ruined and that is enough. I just hope I can endure this fight, soul searching, why? Christmas –I feel like scrooge, Ba Hum Bug! At year end thinking about a fresh start, another year of this? Where are we going? Where will it take us? WHY? I put one foot in front of the other and carry on and survive. Wow, ain't that great. That's all I ever do! I am numb and very tired.

I realized, as I entered 2003, that I was no longer running. In some part due to lack of money. Rehab was my work now. My choice of peer group had gone down hill just like my life had in my estimation. I felt deserted by my friends and started spending time with a guy who just got out of jail. The relationship dissolved but not before I lent him money that I never saw again and he stole my laptop.

The losses were profound! The way I was perceived, abandoned by friends, the man I loved and especially the loss of my dream job. I felt useless because every minute of every day was a reminder due to my tremors, balance, speech and vision. All this work was jeopardized seriously because I began to order alcohol to my home by taxi and drank while my Mom was at work to numb the grief. Recovering from my accident brought my low self-esteem to the surface. I sought out recognition and worth from men because after all, I may not have been able to use my body to dance but I could use it for other things, allowing men to take advantage.

Mom found numerous counselors to assist me with my grieving. I told them what they wanted to hear and didn't engage.

What began to save me was the discovery of a Pilate's studio, a well-respected singing teacher and specialized ABI physiotherapy. The exercises in Pilate's were dance friendly and in singing the vocal exercises were familiar. I started to find the Heather I thought was gone.

Disappointingly my 3 eye surgeries didn't fix everything and to this day I have 11% double vision.

I spent hours writing a screenplay and registered a production company. I met a smooth talker who conned me. I impulsively hired him without a reference check. I paid for classes, bought equipment, leased a car and paid him a salary. I was naïve and trusting. My brain injury had made me extremely vulnerable. I wanted to be master of my own ship so I gave no one power of attorney.

July 14th, 2004. Dr. Wakai told my Mom when they left that the best thank you would be for me to walk back into the hospital in three years and shake his hand. I did that all by myself. "Domo Arigato".

Since then the journey has continued. Writing has given me purpose and has been cathartic and therapeutic. If anything it has saved me a lot of money in counseling. I bear few visible scars and most people are totally unaware of the continuing effects of my accident.

I created a routine, which I call Love Your Body Beautiful. The movements where derived from my knowledge of dance, voice, yoga and Pilate's. I isolate, stretch and strengthen every part of the body. It has been a lifesaver. I feel my body recovering as I execute the exercises. I have shared it with all kinds of people to help them recover the bumps and bruises of life.

The further I move away from the date of my accident the general belief is I look well; therefore all must be well but I will bear invisible scars forever.

Orchid

Kyle McKillop
(December 29, 2013)

She says I am an orchid, bruised

in a humid rainforest.

She leaves warnings:

this will make you cry.

I stretch the length

of my stem, willing

my blank petals to shade,

and blue notes tilt

my ivory beard.

In a quiet hollow, in

secure and wombèd state,

I grow limber

and she, towering, grows

beneath and beyond me.

THE GRAND-MAL LIFE

Julie Reaper with Kim Seary

Thirty years of grand-mal seizures and finally a glimmer of hope in the form of brain surgery.

My name is Julie, and in 2011, I would have a one inch diameter hole drilled through either side of my skull at the temples. My meds would have gradually been decreased a month before the operation in order to induce seizures. Electrodes would be placed directly onto various sections of my naked brain, and I would be in the hospital for ten days with wires attached. My head would be wrapped in layers of gauze. The wires protruding outward would be taped together into a hose-like piece long enough for me to get to the bathroom. These wires would be attached to a machine that would monitor my seizure activity, so that their origin could be detected. Then, with the wires removed from my brain, the skin on my skull would be peeled back from ear to ear. Instruments would then be applied through the holes in my skull to remove the problematic parts of me.

When the neurosurgeon told me all this, it seemed pretty straightforward. I'm a big Star Trek fan - particularly of "Voyager" and especially the character "7 of 9" who is part machine and part human. Under the circumstances, I could relate. After her very dicey separation from the Borg-hive mind, she turned out exceptionally well. I found some comfort in this.

I went and got my head shaved. It felt like an act of liberation and empowerment. Also, everyone thought it looked good.

The week before the surgery was much like a "last meal"; I had to eat special things, and was with my family and best friend the whole time. Thank God for that. I went for lots of long walks, breathing in the sweet smell of the trees or the salt of the ocean. I meditated. I prayed that this operation would be successful. I often wondered if I was making the right decision.

The hardest part about having this illness is never being able to trust oneself completely. I never knew when or where I would have a seizure, and I never remembered them afterwards. My short-term memory would be wiped clean.

When this whole thing began in 1976, at age 18, I was home in Bermuda for the summer holidays. I was at a party when I lost my balance and fell, hitting my head hard on the cement. Everyone heard the crack. I must have passed out for a short time before making my way home and going to bed. I had a headache and felt sick for days, but I didn't tell my parents anything. Of course, in retrospect, I know I suffered a severe concussion.

At first I was mostly having petite-mal seizures during sleep. I would wake with a sore tongue and blood on my pillow. I managed a hip, busy restaurant at the time. My mother insisted I go to the doctor and I was put on medication called Dilantin, which seemed to help. But, as I got older, I would have seizures during the day. I'd fall down, body shaking with tremors – someone would call an ambulance or I would come to half an hour later, sore and groggy, not remembering anything as I made my way home, or went back to whatever it was I was doing before the seizure.

Living in Bermuda, everyone knew me. I enjoyed a modest amount of fame as "The Bird Lady". A friend and I started the "Bermuda Parrot Theatre" at Chrystal Caves, a tourist hot-spot on the island. I had studied operant conditioning as part of my psychology degree in university, so I trained the macaws, cockatoos, and an Amazon parrot how to raise the flag, ride bicycles on wires, roller-skate, and play poker. My friend did the business end. Our show was wildly popular and I grew intimately close to my birds, especially a Malaccan cockatoo named Jocko. The birds all stayed in a little cabin near the tent, but Jocko came home with me. I'd take him back and forth in a cage on my moped and he loved it. He was always on my arm. Because of this recognition, my condition was simply accepted and dealt with calmly. I didn't need to go to the hospital most of the time. People knew to make me comfortable and stay with me until it passed.

In 1992, with my mother's encouragement, I moved to Vancouver where my sister Susan was living. I thought, at the time, if I ever wanted proper help for my epilepsy I would have to go to a larger centre. I was leaving behind friends, family, my birds, and my island home of pink sand and warm turquoise sea. Vancouver was like an alien planet. For one thing, it rained all the time! In Bermuda, people didn't go out in the rain. It took a while for me to clue in and fit myself with rain-gear.

I learned that Jocko pulled out all his feathers after I left. My seizures became worse than ever. It was soon Susan's job to come and pick me up from the hospital every time an ambulance was called by some stranger after witnessing one of my alarming seizures. I went to several GPs, but none of them could get me in to see a specialist. Even CT scans were booked far in advance.

Instead of waiting the five years for a specialist, my mother took me to Calgary to get the scan. It was expensive, and essentially useless. It simply confirmed that I was, indeed, having grand-mal seizures. This was not news to me.

I eventually began having psychotic episodes. I once rented a limo and told the driver to take me to Los Angeles because my brother lived there and was a doctor. I got turned back at the border and wound up in the psych ward. Subsequent visits to various psych wards had me diagnosed as schizophrenic, psychotic, obsessive-compulsive and manic-depressive. I don't remember them even mentioning epilepsy!

I didn't know anyone in Vancouver besides my sister, and felt like an enormous burden. Besides the dozens of hospital pick-ups at all hours of the day and night, she was always very kind and generous – inviting me over for special dinners and calling to check up on me. Although she never complained, I felt bad that I had nothing but my problems to offer her. She was married, working full time and had a child to raise. I met a few people here and there who I would have liked to become friends with, but after seeing me have a seizure, they didn't want anything to do with me. It happened again and again. I became very depressed and tried to commit suicide, and was placed back in the psych ward.

Once, a roommate and I retrieved our clothes and climbed out our window onto the balcony. We shuffled over a few other balconies onto a ladder, climbed down, and went to the nearest store. We bought cigarettes and smoked a few before sneaking back up to our room. We couldn't believe it! No one even realized we were gone! We began to do this regularly and the thrill of getting away with it, as well as having fun while we were out there, definitely helped in keeping me sane. In the meantime, it seemed as if I was being tested with just about every medication there was. Finally, doctors found one they thought would help me, and then I was released.

Eventually, with this new medication, I was able to return to school to study counseling. I already had my bachelor's in psychology. Meeting new people and learning helped me regain some balance in my life. However, my seizures changed once again, I began sleepwalking. I would unconsciously get up out of bed, dress myself, and walk out the door. I only remember waking up and reading the nearest street sign so I could orient myself and find my way home. Thank goodness for the mystery of unconscious survival skills. Anything could have happened to me on those walks! I finally moved to a place with a chain padlock on the inside so I was able to lock myself in.

In spite of my memory problems, I graduated as a Registered Counselor and Certified Clinical Hypnotherapist in 1999. I was ecstatic! I rented an office and got all set up before realizing it was all too much. I wasn't going to be able to trust myself enough to practice counseling. My seizures were becoming more frequent and dangerous. When I fell, I was injuring myself badly. Life became a living hell and I was desperate for some measure of dignity and autonomy. So, in September of 2001, I got a job in telephone sales for the Vancouver Symphony.

While sitting at fiberglass classroom desks in a cramped, airless room, being trained in the complexities of phone sales, a woman three rows up from me began crumpling pieces of paper. When "the teacher" wasn't looking, she threw them at the heads of other potential phone-room employees. It was pretty funny. At the break she approached me and told me she could see my aura. She said it was turquoise and pink. I met her after work, and we walked back to our homes across the Burrard Bridge. The aurora borealis lit up the night - a wonder of green light dancing through the summer sky. I took it as a sign of good things to come.

This creative, beautiful, crazy woman named Kim was the first and only person who accepted me despite my epilepsy. And although I was still tentative, I dared to hope I had finally met a friend. I prayed fervently for this fragile seed of a relationship to take root and grow. My prayers were answered and truth be told, if it weren't for her love and faith, as well as the support of my mother and sister, I quite literally would not have survived.

One of the things that bonded Kim and I early on, was art. With her encouragement, we did oil pastel pictures together without regard for whether or not they were "good". Eventually, on my own, I experienced the deep healing power of drawing dozens of butterflies with pencil crayons. In 2010, she and I started a group for people with mental health issues called Spirit Art.

It's been two and a half years since my surgery. There are scars and bumps on my skull, but they are covered by my hair, which has grown past my shoulders, and is curlier than before. Everyone says it looks good. I have a dent in my head on the right side which I wear with pride. I have a little balcony in my apartment that I've painted turquoise, and I often walk at sunset so that I am bathed in pink. I've had a few seizures since the surgery, but nothing so severe as in the past. The inner healing is moving more slowly now. I'm learning about myself - learning how to deal with emotions. The illness had always taken care of that for me, suppressing severe emotions with seizures.

There are all these big and confusing feelings to deal with, but I'm holding on – staying sane while life moves at me. Structure. God. Love. Faith. Hope. Nature – I am reborn, I rebuild. I have always trusted that it happened for a reason. When people asked me what I did for a living, I'd tell them I was a "universal researcher". But I was hiding too – wanting to stay in my shell so I could feel safe. It's been a lonely existence.

Now I am daring to see that my life is about thriving, when, for so long, it seemed solely about surviving. My best friend, Kim, and I went to Bowen Island on Sunday and walked the four kilometers around Killarney lake. Everywhere we looked, we were struck by the wonder of tall trees with their long-legged vertical roots. Over time, they'd transformed into sturdy trunks straddling murdered rotting stumps– life flourishing impossibly from death and destruction, with wild, sweet birdsong all around. That is me, now. La vie douce…et fort.

Julie Reaper

I Do...

A story by Kim for Julie at Christmas
December of 2009
Kim Seary

I remember the first time she fell down and bled. I was pretty sure it was just a scrape on her elbow, but it was dark in that pot-holed parking lot behind Videomatica. We'd been inside for too long, poking around indecisively about what we wanted to see, sweating in our outdoor clothes.

Until that night, she'd been strangely secretive with me, offering only little hints about herself and her life; why she didn't have a good job, even though she was well educated; why she was so tentative with other people.

She told me she didn't have any friends and I couldn't fathom why. She was so beautiful; caramel-coloured hair and eyes, a lithe, athletic body, and a voice full of warmth. She radiated a profound gentleness that made hers a lovely energy to be near. Like suddenly coming upon a wild deer in the forest, I felt I'd been unexpectedly blessed with her tender appearance.

We worked together for several weeks in the telephone sales room for the symphony. That's where we met. One night, we were given free tickets. I sat and put a program on the empty seat beside me and held my breath until she joined me. Just as the lights were dimming, she flashed me a fragile butterfly smile, and asked me if I sang.

"There was a time when I couldn't speak… I could only sing." She said. I was completely mesmerized.

From then on, after work, we'd walk home across the bridge together and sing pop tunes or I'd mock the phone room scene, and she'd thank me, saying she really needed to laugh.

I wanted her to be my friend. I suppose I was in love with her. Who was this enigmatic, unearthly creature? I was more than half-convinced she was an angel of some sort.

So now here she was, in the dirt and pools of car excrement behind the video store. Nothing could be more wrong. For a second, I was overwhelmed with panic. Should I go get help? I couldn't just leave her there alone. I did something, then, that felt perfectly right. I lay down beside her, and stroked her hair and her back, and said over and over, "You're alright. You are with me. I love you. You're alright."

I don't know how much time passed - probably a few minutes. She sat up and tried and take off her coat and shoes. She was talking, but it didn't seem to make any sense. I thought then that I should leave her and run inside to call an ambulance, but she stood, brushed herself off and asked, "Did I fall?"

"Yes." I said.

"Where are we?" she wondered.

"We're going to my place to watch a movie." I told her.

"Oh, good" she said, and started to walk as if nothing had happened.

Later, when we were cleaning up her cuts, she told me about her epilepsy and how people who saw her have seizures were scared and didn't want to have anything to do with her again.

"I do." I said.

Taxi Cabs and Snow Globes

Kim Fink-Jenson

Journal entry: December 2013

I'm adrift. Life after my accident is disconnected from life before. Things seem unreal, they don't quite make sense or match up at the edges. A shift into a parallel, nightmarish reality. I have no tolerance. My mind runs in irrational directions. I'm not connected,

I feel so alone. If only I could remember what happened, maybe all this would make sense.

I doubt myself, because outside I look fine. Only I experience the headaches, the confusion, the dizziness, the anxiety, the growing sense of panic in bright lights, crowds, noise. Only I burst into tears, run from the store, cart abandoned in the aisle to take refuge in a quiet car. Only I leave the party early because too many conversations collide. No one else sees it or feels it, so I ask myself, shouldn't I be better by now? Am I weak? Am I making this up? But these changes are real.

❋　❋　❋　❋

While crossing the street with my husband and two friends, I was hit by a cab. A blur of yellow, a raised hand to stop it, and then a dazed recollection of a familiar voice sounding panicked, yelling at the 911 operator, "Police AND ambulance. Someone was just hit by a car." I wonder who? Sitting on the curb, sore, shaken. Oh. Me.

No, I didn't hit my head. No, I don't think I was unconscious at any point. (Was I?) Yes, an icepack would be nice. My shoulder and neck are very sore. Jokes in the ambulance, trying to make light. We were out for a night of celebration. I didn't want to make more of it than it was. I had walked myself to the ambulance, after all. Couldn't be that bad. We had dinner reservations to get to… The menu didn't make sense, so I let everyone else order. I laughed it off. What a crazy start to the night!

Two and a half weeks and three doctors later, someone finally put the pieces together and diagnosed a mild traumatic brain injury. I was terrified. I was three months into my PhD in Rehabilitation Sciences working, ironically, on a project about students with disabilities. Now I was experiencing academic challenges from the inside. Words swam on the page and refused to make sense, scrolling a computer screen gave me vertigo. I couldn't find words to express myself. I got lost in familiar places. Time slipped through my fingers and deadlines passed before I'd even started a task or realized I'd be late. I couldn't prioritize the many demands on my time.

My kids were loud and moved too much. I yelled at them to be quiet and sit still. I'd find myself standing in the kitchen in tears, bewildered by how to make dinner. I didn't want to get out of bed in the morning because there, for a few precious moments, I might feel okay, but as my day slogged on, I felt worse and worse. I spent most of that first month lying down in a darkened room, crying from fear, depression, the pain in my head and body, drifting in and out of dream-filled sleep.

❦　❦　❦　❦

Email to friends and family: March 2014

I am in such a negative space, not trusting and not liking myself. I can't hear what people have to say and have it be constructive. All I can hear is stuff that feeds self-negativity. I know you're trying to help. I do want to hear what you have to say, but I can't hear it right now.

I am sorry too that right now I am not supportive or appreciative enough of those I love. I am sorry if the words come out wrong or I haven't said anything good about you in a while. It's hard to see someone else's needs for positive feedback when you can't find a positive thought for yourself.

I know this is hard for you too. Know that I am trying my best and I love you. Sometimes, I say things that come out harsh, I don't always recognize it, but things come out wrong and sound more negative or sarcastic than I mean. I can be dark and sad and I'm not much fun to be around. I'm sorry. I'm working on it. I ask for your patience on this bumpy road.

❦　❦　❦　❦

I'm getting better, but the last six months have been the hardest months of my life. There are times when I doubt everything: my schooling, my career, my marriage, my ability to be a mother, my relationships. I just want to run far away from it all, far away from responsibility, far away from the unintentional hurt I cause other people, far away from the disappointment I feel I've become to those around me.

I try to keep up, hide the challenges I'm having. But everything is overwhelming and hard. Classes are exhausting. My bum is in the seat but the fluorescent lights make my headaches and confusion worse. Beyond the first half hour of class, I can't absorb anything. At the end of the school day, I fall into my bed exhausted and nap for several hours before making dinner, eating, and returning to bed. Luckily, I only have classes two days a week, Monday and Tuesday. But by the end of Tuesday, I am so exhausted and confused, it takes me until Monday to recover just to repeat it again.

I met another student with a brain injury and we laughed and commiserated about how uninjured people just don't get it. Aren't grocery stores the worst!? Riding sideways on transit? I know, right? Absolutely nauseating.

❧　　❧　　❧　　❧

Concussion Clinic: January 2014

"Imagine your head is like a snow globe. Before your concussion the water was clear, all the snowflakes were settled. When you were concussed, the snow globe got a mighty shake and all the snow was swirling around, making it hard to think clearly. It takes time for the snow to settle again. Problem is, now that it's been shaken, anything – stress, overstimulation, noise, bright lights, tasks requiring focus – can shake the snow globe again."

After three months of trying to cope and live as if the snow would settle any day, I hit rock bottom. Even with physical therapy, vestibular therapy, and post-traumatic counseling, I just didn't seem to be getting any better. I had to resign from my research assistantship. I had to cancel presenting at a conference in Japan. For the first time in my life I needed extensions on assignments and special accommodations in the classroom. I was struggling with day-to-day tasks at home. I slid deeper and deeper into depression. I was desperate.

My doctor put me on antidepressants and I continued to work through the accident with my therapist. There were some very, very dark days but finally, the medication has started to help enough that I can function again.

With a more positive mood, I cope better with the remaining symptoms of the concussion and physical injuries. I take it moment-to-moment, not day-to-day. I respect that I need to take things slowly and say no to extra demands. I accept that smartphone alarms and GPS are my greatest friends. And I know this experience has given me an inside look, a deeper understanding of the challenges others face.

There are moments when life is quiet that I almost feel normal. But there are still days like today at my daughter's orchestra performance when the crowd and the noise and the motion around me are too much. Hands shaking, heart pounding, thoughts swirling in undefined panic, I run for the fresh air and bird song in the pouring rain outside the auditorium. I take a deep breath, or ten, and remember I'm still recovering. I close my eyes, water dripping from my hair, and wait for the swirling snow to fall.

Not Just a Headline

Jenny Callaghan

People say to us: "But you look fine!"

No scars, no obviously missing pieces.

When they say that, they don't mean badly: they want us to be well. No one wants to hear that you may never work again or drive a car or remember what you did yesterday. Brain injury is the invisible injury. Nobody understands what enormous effort it's taking you to nod and smile and look as if you really are following the conversation and are going to remember every word they have said.

In the first few months after the accident, when I was standing, I was tilted to the left: not tilted enough to fall over, just enough to look as if I might do so at any minute. Sometimes, after staring at me for a while, a person might mention tactfully that I was tilted to the left but of course, I didn't believe them. Why would I? I knew that I was standing completely, evenly upright and that everyone around me was tilting over to the right. I didn't know why they would do that, and really, I didn't even wonder why. That was just how people were.

One day, giggling, the nurses in the rehab hospital dragged over a full-length mirror to show me that I was tilted to the left. Well blow me down with a feather! They were right. Then they pushed down on my right shoulder to even me up but that made me feel as if I was going to fall over. From then on I had to remember each day to tilt a little bit to the right so that other people would be satisfied that I was upright. Anything to please.

It took a long time to learn where upright was. I found my mind wandering when people talked to me as I concentrated on the tipping game: was this tilt enough to satisfy them, or was it maybe a tad too much? Would they notice? Would I fall over?

You look as "normal" as everyone else, whatever that means. When you do something odd – for example, opening the door that leads into the coat closet instead of the door that exits the building, or calling a cup a duck, or one of those sorts of things you do – it's no use your saying, "Oh but you see, actually, there's this thing wrong with me…."

I've tried that. There's an interested silence and you are the focus of their attention for a split second while they wait for an explanation. A jumble of words and images go through my mind, as I try to figure out which one of them to pick up, where to start. "You see, we were turning left….." I begin. Sometimes I continue with the whole story, the quiet country road, the speeding truck, the waking up a week later….. Usually eyes glaze over before I get too far.

"How are you?" elicits the same long-winded and literal response. I tell people every detail of how I am that day and sometimes all about yesterday and last week as well. Only when people start to drift away from me does it occur to me something is wrong though I don't know what it is. Brain doesn't understand what they need to know or what I need to tell them.

My therapist had me write down the answer to these common questions on a piece of paper which I was to carry with me in my pocket. Well, can you imagine yourself at some social gathering asking someone how they are or what is wrong with them and then, sympathetically, how that happened. The person, me, stares into space for a while, trying to remember what I am supposed to do. Then I start to dig into my pocket and after some time, pull out a piece of paper from which I read slowly like a five-year old in class. "My brain was injured in a car accident." I smile with a sense of accomplishment.

I couldn't keep up with conversations. I couldn't find the right words because they were hidden in boxes in the dark on my mind's floor. The boxes had no labels. There was no way of telling what was inside them. If I wanted not to make mistakes, I just had to take the time to pick up a box and unwrap it and see if it was the right one. I often had to unwrap two or three boxes before I found the right one. By that time the conversation around me had usually had moved on to the weather or the latest movie. I was always five minutes behind. I would want to put my hand up as if I was in grade school and say, "My turn, my turn!" But it was too late.

I seemed to have fewer words than I used to have and the wrong words kept popping up in their place. I once announced that my cat's hair was full of knots and I might have to take him to get pruned. Another time, sitting in the park, I saw a dragonfly hovering over the grass, "Look, a purple helicopter!" I said.

My brain had become focused on me. Other people's lives were irrelevant, as for the most part, were their feelings. Instead of asking, "Would you mind lowering your voice?" It came out as, "Quiet!" The extra words that changed the tone from a request to an angry command were quite beyond me, and anyway I didn't care about how people felt. I was too tired that moment to search for the extra words in those packets on the floor of my brain. All that I could retrieve were the bones of a sentence, not the flesh or the clothes.

I found it almost impossible to get to the point. I couldn't have explained why: just that's how it was. Explaining something was like being in a maze and taking the wrong turns all the time. Like Alice in Wonderland, I could see the garden gate I wanted to get to but not how to get there. I turned and wandered and rambled and repeated myself and sometimes just never got where I was headed. My therapist, when I started doing that to him would say: "Start at the end." Sometimes that worked.

The first few months after my accident were just a thick cloud of confusion, a daily struggle. To everyone around me I was baffling and unpredictable. How I seemed to other people, however, was something which never once crossed my mind. All of my energies were spent figuring out how to get through the day, and learning important things like how to cross the road. Self-absorbed as I was and limited in energy, it was more than I could manage to think of my illness from anyone else's perspective. People around me could see that my behaviour and judgment had changed. I couldn't. I was totally lacking in self-awareness, oblivious to how I was behaving, not seeing how my brain injury was distorting how I saw things. Professionals familiar with brain injury call it: "lack of insight." If someone had said to me that I lacked "insight" into my behaviour, I would have disagreed ferociously with them. The way I saw life was the way it was. I was right and everyone else was wrong. I was upright and they were tilting sideways. Obviously. They were just being extraordinarily difficult. I had no way of stepping outside of my damaged brain to see my behaviour from the outside. I didn't have an undamaged brain with which to do that.

At the beginning I used to call my brain injury a "head injury." It sounded less catastrophic, gentler and more ordinary, as in, "I banged my head!" It sounded like something that happens to everyone, something that would get better soon.

I didn't want to use words that suggested I was really different from everyone else or that I couldn't cope. I wanted to be the same as them, someone with perhaps just a wee bit of a challenge to overcome. Of course, the truth was that I couldn't cope at all. I couldn't go out by myself, couldn't read properly or write, couldn't shop, sleep, manage money, cross roads, drive: the list goes on.

My brain had become very literal. I understood everything in concrete terms and occasionally, even now, when Brain is tired, it falls back into that mode. When asked, "How did you get a brain injury?" I begin again:

"Well you see we were turning left…."

When I'm with several people and jokes are made quickly, I often misunderstand: I take a joking comment as a literal statement. A chicken? Crossing a road? By itself? Which road, where?

Brain began to seem not part of me, as in, "My Brain," but like a two-year old in my care that I had to watch over at all times. A two-year-old might run across the road without looking or tell a stranger in the elevator that he didn't like her hat. As my daughter used to say to me reassuringly, "That wasn't you, Momma, it was your brain". That would be hard to explain to the stranger in the elevator. There was the Real Me and then there was this unruly two-year-old who had taken over. The "Real Me," might the next day feel awful about Brain's behaviour, but it's not as if I could leave him at home.

In the tiny and lonely world inside my head, I couldn't think of the consequences of my actions, I couldn't think of other people's feelings, I couldn't judge the appropriateness of what I was saying, I didn't think much about right and wrong. Or at least Brain couldn't. I couldn't see the "big picture" which is what you need to see to make sound choices and ethical decisions. When a neighbour talked too much and wouldn't go home and I was at the end of my tether with fatigue, I had a really strong urge to stick something sharp in her bare arm. If I could have seen the big picture, I would have seen that, well, she might just call the police. I might also have considered that it would hurt her and that there might be other ways of persuading her to go home. I might see that mine was not normal, neighbourly behaviour. I lacked self-control and I lacked empathy but didn't know that. I couldn't think about how she might be feeling. I also couldn't see that I needed my friendly neighbours and that she was only being kind, thinking that I'd enjoy her company. If I could have seen the big picture I might have seen that what I wanted to do was appalling. I could only feel my own mounting panic as she talked on and on, oblivious to the fact that Brain was understanding less and less, oblivious to my very real fears of having a seizure.

When now I remember my behaviour of those first few years, I cringe: the impulse decisions, the unprovoked outbursts of temper. The physiatrist (the rehabilitation doctor) who was treating me reassured me that this was par for the course, that people with brain injuries often had "a short fuse," in his words. Mine felt very short. I would blow suddenly and without warning. These explosions didn't feel like it does when you lose your temper, where there is a feeling of mounting anger that you can choose to control, to channel, suppress (or lose). My explosions were as uncontrollable as a sneeze: something physical and completely unmanageable. Actually, even a sneeze can be "felt" before it arrives. These eruptions came from nowhere or so it seemed at the time and they astonished me as much as they astonished the unfortunate people around me.

In my mind, I simply thought that everyone around me was being demanding and patronizing, ignoring my needs and adding to, if not causing, my difficulties. It didn't occur to me that there might other ways of dealing with things other than to yell at people, loudly. It was quite some time, maybe a couple of years before it occurred to me that people were not really being unreasonable: in fact, most people were incredibly kind.

I have awful memories of some of these outbursts: the time when upset by hours of hammering, I flung the back door open and swore quite fluently at the people renovating the house next door; the awful incident in a restaurant when for no apparent reason I yelled so loudly at my daughter that she burst into tears and everyone stopped eating, forks suspended in mid-air, to watch the performance; the occasion I exploded into verbal abuse at the home help because her phone conversation was a touch loud.

Despite all my problems I really thought that one day I would wake up and be "better" (whatever that means) return to my job, which I loved, be "normal" (whatever that means) as well. Getting better for me meant returning to my old life, returning to work particularly. A lot of my identity was wrapped up in what I did for a living. This is true for lots of us. How often have you been asked by someone you have just met, "And what do you do?"

I could never again think of a good answer to that question. I see doctors? I'm learning to read? I'm trying really, really hard to walk in a straight line?

In so many ways a brain injury changes who you are.

After many years of living with a brain injury I show little signs of anything wrong unless I'm over-tired, only suffering from sleeplessness, an occasional inability to find my way around in new places and a habit of telling the same stories over and over again.

Many people with brain injuries would be unable to write the book I have been trying to write. On the other hand, it has taken 15 years so far. I'd hate you to think that all that writing was done in a week or that doing it came easily to a person with a brain injury. You should see the first 115 drafts.

Ceiling Fan, Concussion

(recorded in bed on December 4, 2013, 13 days after a mild head injury)

Kyle McKillop

To the ceiling fan overhead
as I lie here concussed:
you are so boring to watch.

You have five points
like a starfish,
those three beaded cords
like octopus legs.

No one knows which cords
are meant to spin you
or turn on your light.

Seriously,
ceiling fan designers,
grow the hell up
and put some labels
on your products.
Thank you.

Strange Ghost in a Faulty Machine

Susan Cormier

Spring 1992

At sixteen, I have had thirteen years of music lessons, started shortly after my mother realized I had learned to read. Teachers and tests tell me I am unusually bright, but I pay little attention in school. I read psychological thrillers, write despondent songs. I am socially clumsy, thrift-store-bedraggled, rendered invisible by years of schoolyard bullying. Counselors scribble concerned notes about "self-mutilation" and "chronic depression" but are at a loss about what to do with me. I am quietly angry, and overwhelmingly sad. "Hope" is not something I believe in.

If I could time travel and reassure my former teenage self that everything would eventually turn out okay, that one day she would be happy, confident, and overwhelmingly glad to be alive, I would not. Knowing what the next year and beyond held in store for her would have broken what little spirit she had.

March 27, evening

Road turns right, car veers left. A skid of gravel, thump – flashing lights, spinning trees.

Silence. The stench of gasoline.

My head is pinned; ceiling carpet grates my cheek. Something so heavy is crushing me – I breathe small, gasping. I strain my eyes towards the driver – open door, empty seat.

I only remember flashes of the time between a few minutes before the accident and several days after. This memory loss was attributed by various doctors to shock and trauma, the opiate painkillers I received in the hospital, or from getting "quite a knock on the head."

March 28, early morning

I am strapped to an uncomfortably hard surface while a nurse picks glass shards out of my hand. A puzzle-piece-shaped blank spot obscures part of her face. It is neither white, nor black, nor grey, nor textured, simply an indescribable space where there is nothing to see.

"Nurse, I can't see you."

She leans towards my face. The blank spot replicates, spreads.

The last corner of vision blips into blankness and I yell, "Nurse! I can't see you!"

Hands touch me; a voice calls for a doctor. I open my eyes wide as I can and squeeze them shut, blink – nothing. Not black, white, or grey, just – nothing.

I do not know how long the blindness lasted. For several days I was semicomatose, and recall little. The blindness was attributed to shock and/or chemical poisoning due to the amount of gasoline I'd absorbed through my skin. It is also a symptom of brain trauma.

March 31

I regain enough consciousness to ask about my injuries; they are listed off like organs on an anatomy chart. Collapsed lung. Bleeding kidneys. Chemical burn from collarbone to knees. Loose teeth, saved only by my orthodontic braces. Broken bones: hips, pelvis, sternum, half my ribs.

Feeling something beneath my head, I reach behind and feel a lump, big enough that my cupped hand does not cover it. "Oh, and a concussion," I am told, as an afterthought.

Early April

After I am moved from Intensive Care to a regular ward, my mother brings me a few items to keep me occupied.

I'd previously had a reading level far beyond my years, but find books dull and complicated. I force myself to read a page or two at a time, but from one day to the next cannot remember what I've read.

I scrawl in my journal with large, childlike handwriting, almost entirely in capitals. I turn the radio on; it is noisy and complicated. I turn it off; the silence and muffled hospital noises are suffocating. I am irritable, restless.

Mid-April

Mobile on crutches, I return home, and find myself disoriented in a strange building. I climb out of bed, and am lost in a corner of my room. The hands of my clock show odd times – eight o'clock, no, four. Everything tastes like something else: bottled water like the scent of wet dog, lettuce like rich black mud.

I scribble in my journal:

"I must've damaged my taste buds when I bit open my tongue, and the inside of my nose was probably baked from the gasoline. Everything tastes salty, except milk which tastes sour....My wallet smells like gasoline to my mom, but to me it smells like neat's-foot oil. Our bottle of neat's-foot oil smells like pine-scented floor cleaner."

After a few days of disorientation, I conclude my right/left perception has gotten scrambled, my senses are…confused. I learn to move slowly, to stare at things as I figure them out, to trust my hands more than my eyes. I learn to approach foods and scented objects as though I have never encountered them before, to build new opinions of what I do and do not like.

I mention my odd sensory perceptions to doctors. They are unsurprised, unconcerned. "You did," I am told repeatedly, "get quite the bump on the head."

Late April

The handwriting in my school notebooks is foreign yet familiar, something from a dream. I am fascinated by the words in my own handwriting – "I know this? Really?" My memories of a few weeks previous resurface as though buried under years of time – wistful and nostalgic, details hazy and lost.

After weeks of long slow days, of sleeping between doctors' appointments and struggling to understand homeschooled lessons, I return to school.

Encountering acquaintances that I haven't seen since before the accident is like rediscovering favourite books. I laugh, marvel at their stories, find their personalities fascinating. Some comment on how happy I am. One queries whether I am on drugs.

I describe how bizarre it is to have been one day fully-functioning and alive, then the next incapacitated, immobile, in crippling pain – how incredibly happy I am to slowly relearn how to move about, how to do simple things. My attempts to explain meet with baffled looks from my teenaged friends.

Although I still struggle with depression, since the car accident I have never again experienced the despondent psychological immobility that plagued my teenage years. Regardless of my life adventures, my head no longer says, "I can't do this," but rather, "How am I going to do this?"

Perhaps my extreme change in attitude was due to having survived a brush with death. Perhaps it was due to having gotten "quite a knock on the head." I don't believe I need to know.

May

In choir, I am surprised but not alarmed by my inability to read music. Although I'd studied music for years, the lines and dots of music notation are now meaningless to me. Recalling my slow struggle to relearn the symbols of math – a subject I'd previously excelled in -- I listen carefully to those around me and follow their voices as we sing, confident that my musical knowledge will return.

Unlike mathematics, which I was required to relearn in order to graduate school, reading music was not something I had to focus on in the months during my recovery. I never regained my ability to read or play music. I still write songs in my head, but have no way to transcribe them. I write them as poems, stories, and sing a cappella to myself, in odd keys.

Summer

I express concern to a doctor that my memory is much poorer than before. He gives me a list of ten words to memorize. When he later asks me to recall the words, I can only remember seven. Six, he says, is the average rate of recall, ergo in my case no memory loss is indicated.

This was the only medical test of my mental capabilities I had after the accident. It was nearly twenty years before a CT scan, an MRI, or any other exam was done to ascertain what damage if any had been done to my brain.

Fall

Tired of hearing the dismissive, "Well, you did have a concussion," I give up reporting my concerns about cognitive problems to my doctors. Specialists express concern about the healing of my bones, flesh, skin – not about my brain, the most delicate and important organ in my body. The connection between the car accident and my cognitive symptoms is acknowledged, but not addressed in either medical treatment or the car accident lawsuit.

I learn to expect strange things from my head, to catalogue my awareness of my mind alongside my awareness of my body – as something observable and separate from my self, a strange ghost in a faulty machine, unusual and unpredictable.

1994

In conversation with a college classmate, I suddenly find myself unable to speak. Midsentence, I can only make a choking, gargling noise while flapping my hands ineffectively. I stop, swallow – but cannot say a word.

This happens repeatedly that year – I forget how to speak, how to translate my thoughts into words. The more I focus on what I am trying to say, the harder it is to talk.

Eventually, I figure out a coping tactic: immediately say something else. Compliment someone's shirt, recite a line from a poem – anything unrelated to what I am actually trying to say somehow distracts my brain and enables me to speak.

The occurrence of speech difficulties continues throughout my life. Sometimes the problem is a single word. I unintentionally substitute a word for one related in spelling or meaning – 'paint' for 'pain', or 'teacher' for 'school'. Other times I babble nonsensical strings of words, sentences without meaning, as I try to force my way through a sporadic, spontaneous inability to vocalize nouns.

Broca's aphasia is a language disorder characterized by a disturbance in the ability to use words to communicate. It is caused by a brain dysfunction, typically a stroke, lesion, or hemorrhage in the left hemisphere. There is no cure, only therapeutic treatment.

1997

I am watching an intellectual thriller movie. The volume is loud, the plot engaging.

I suddenly feel inexplicably exhausted. I peer at the movie which seems suddenly strange and disjointed. I realize a half hour or more has passed without my knowledge. I have not been asleep – but I have somehow been unconscious, or unaware.

This scenario repeats itself a decade later: someone I am watching television with nudges me and says my name – which usually wakes me from even a deep sleep – but I remain unresponsive until I suddenly regain awareness a half hour later. Five years thereafter, in a theatre with a friend, I again feel that sudden overwhelming exhaustion, and fight to maintain consciousness through the show.

I've never found a medical explanation for these seizure-like episodes – aside from, of course, the usual acknowledgement that while in my teens, I did get "quite a bump on the head".

2005

At work, I am helping two customers pick out an item. I rest my hand against a shelf and wait to see if they have any questions.

I am in a virtual space, surrounded by walls and bars of bold red and black as lines of numbers and words flow around me. Voices move through space like objects as I slide between large dark cubes and gliding walls.

The store's shelf is cold and angular beneath my hand. I have been dreaming, or hallucinating. I cannot judge by the customers' faces whether I've been gone several minutes or half a moment. I stammer something politely generic, and walk away.

I have never knowingly ingested any hallucinogen. My only guess as to the nature of this episode is some kind of spontaneous occurrence of delta brainwaves. I have heard of micro sleeps, where a person loses consciousness for a fraction of a second...but micro dreams?

Spring 2008

While riding public transit, I suddenly become hyperaware of the interconnected relativity of all that exists. All the seemingly random details of the world – explosions on the morning news, my cat's preference for tuna – are arranged in a perfectly logical, incredibly beautiful four-dimensional pattern.

I somehow know that as moments pass, this awareness will decrease, and trying to write it down will make it fade faster. So I sit quietly, staring out the window at the morning sunlight, amazed at how everything in existence fits together so perfectly.

It fades slowly, like a waking dream. Within minutes, I only recall a vague diagram of a double helix covered in lights with overlapping beams.

Dream, hallucination, vision? Was my brain misfiring…again? This remains the most beautiful and profound moment of my life. I have never been able to name what I experienced, but I carry the assurance that somehow, it all makes sense: everything has meaning and purpose, even if I only understood it for a moment.

October 2010

I am momentarily dazzled by a bright light. Minutes later, one eye loses sight, and the other's vision is rippled and watery, mottled with bright arcs of colour. Alarmed, I call a doctor who urges me to get to an emergency room, fearing a stroke or some optical emergency. My sight returns within an hour, and hospital doctors find nothing wrong with me.

This episode – minus the trip to the emergency room – repeats hundreds of times in the next few years. With each episode the visual symptoms diminish, but are replaced with cognitive and behavioural symptoms including confusion, memory loss, and irritability.

Two years of neurologist appointments, MRIs, and CT scans pass. My tests show nothing: no lesion, scarring, tumour, or evidence of brain injury. In the absence of any other medical evidence, my diagnosis is Silent Complicated Migraine. Cause: unknown.

I struggle constantly with these odd episodes that range from momentary confusion to hours of comprehension problems and acute irritability. It is difficult to explain to others that what they see as random fits of short-tempered impatience is a medical problem with a vague and possibly inaccurate diagnosis. I wish I could wear a bracelet that reads, "Please have patience with me. My brain does strange things. I'm doing the best I can."

2015

Twenty-four years ago, I received a diagnosis of concussion, but no treatment for brain trauma was given, nor was any concern for possible brain damage expressed. Now, no physical observable evidence of any brain injury has been found using current medical techniques. I remain certain that the trauma to my brain changed who I was, changed how my mind worked and how I experienced the world. There is no medical evidence for this.

My body and brain are idiosyncratic characters I share my life with. One is arthritic and riddled with scar tissue and mishealed injuries, yet still surprises me by carrying me throughout the day. The other is a complex machine that misfires and malfunctions in inexplicable ways, yet somehow keeps my entire body alive. It does strange things, sometimes. I don't know why.

I have no assurance of what will happen to me as I grow older.

As seen in many survivors of strokes and aneurysms, brain trauma can result in distinct changes in behaviour, personality and attitude. Perhaps my thirst for life and the incredible joy and delight I feel about the world is the result of having survived a near-death experience. Or perhaps it's due to having sustained quite a knock on the noggin, a bump that jostled part of my brain. I don't believe I need to know.

THE BREAK

Jude Neale

I fell back arse over tit, lost my composure and clawed at the air as I plummeted down to the cement basketball court. I landed like a lame bird surrounded by my classmates.

Ankles.

Calves.

Knees.

Thighs.

Waist.

Neck.

The game of skill, bravery and bravado known as Chinese Skip consisted of a large circular elastic band and girls who wanted to scale the social echelons of class. I was one of those girls.

I didn't have any friends yet and it was important I prove myself in this universal jumping game. I wanted the folded white notes ripped out of books in class or the meaningful arch of a butterfly eyebrows. Let me be someone else. Not always "the twin".

I walked round and round the school with the duty teacher at recess so that I didn't feel so nakedly alone. This was the year my brother had given me up for a pair of buck-toothed boys who called me Fred. I was forced to watch the world and its subterran ean machinations, so I responded only in tentative nods.

I'd seen the bigger girls doing it, daring each other to jump higher over the stretched elastic until someone fumbled and laughingly dropped out of the game. If I could do that, I would b e popular too. I would have my own fabulous identity. So I asked Mom for elastic, tied the knotted circle to the basement door handle and a chair, and began to practice.

I was bold and athletic. In the days that I trained, I teetered on the tips of my toes before landing lightly inside the quivering circle higher than my waist. I was ready. I packed up my equipment for the morning and dreamed big dreams in my new twinless bedroom.

I woke up to the thump of my Dad's hand on the door telling me to "Rouse, you lazy scoundrel!"

Underwear. Sweater. Skirt. Knee socks. Oxfords. I raced to the kitchen to eat the customary porridge with raisins and brown sugar. It was ballast for my suppressed joy.

Jude, oh you MUST know, Jude! By twelve thirty today all the school would be saying that.

I grabbed my tin lunchbox off the counter and headed for the door. I knew that things would never be the same.

I raced through the ravine and along the quiet road to get to my low slung Departure Bay Elementary School. The bell rang and I felt ready. Like a racehorse, my Granddad would say. I found the hook for my Hudson's Bay coat, clearly labeled Judy by my unwhimsical teacher, and sat down.

Arithmetic first, a terrible torture. No Pencil. No Brain. Then, social studies. Where was England anyway? Why did someone draw a moustache on Her Majesty's face at the back of the classroom? I watched the clock until the bell clanged and I rejoiced, running outside purposefully with the other kids.

It was time. Now. Before the lines got too long. I joined a group of curious girls and felt like a Trojan Horse. The kind my brother had taught me to be. Low key and casual, I asked if I could play. They faintly nodded. First the blonde, then the brainy one and then me. They sang and I jumped in and out of the circle until the elastic came up to my knees. I was smiling, triumphant, until I tripped and cartwheeled backwards to the ground.

I felt the hard cold concrete and then nothing. Only blackness and faraway voices. Then the cool press of my teacher's fingers upon my wrist. I woke in an ambulance with the sirens screaming. I was happy to have made such a memorable exit. I'd made an impact all right. My own memory was gone, truly a terrible thing when you can't study for tests, remember your own phone number, or even the lyrics to a favourite song.

I spent four weeks in hospital where the bump on my skull grew to enormous proportions. Just a fracture, just a concussion, said the medical staff. They studied my x-rays and traced their fingers along the fissure so I could see it, too.

I vomited and moaned when I moved. Ate the green jello and pushed everything else away. Deep sleep and my stuffie named Macduff watching over me. I made new dream memories so I could see myself tripping lightly out of the game at the neck. But the truth was I needed a long time to find six letter words for scrabble and I smiled at entire conversations with blue unfocused eyes.

Mom and Dad cosseted with bottles of Bick's dill pickles and Nancy Drew books. The class had to write letters on blue-ruled foolscap to tell me how much they missed me. One of them even told me that the game was now unfortunately banned.

I recovered slowly. Voices were quiet and it was clear that I had been a very lucky girl. Surely, now, they would say: Jude, oh you MUST know Jude!

JEFF CORNESS

As told to Nicole Nozick

In the winter of 1995, celebrated BC composer and choreographer Jeff Corness and his colleague, Karen Jamieson traveled to the BC interior to meet with members of the Gitxsan band. Jeff and Karen were working on a new interdisciplinary piece that centered on cultural differences in the modern world. They hoped to collaborate on the project with the First Nations band by featuring traditional Gitxsan performers as a central part of the piece. The performance they were working on was part of a larger show, Stone Soup, scheduled to debut in the spring.

On their return trip from the Gitanmaax reserve, the car skidded on black ice and was broadsided by a large pickup truck. Both Jeff and Karen were severely injured and medevac'd to Vancouver General Hospital. Jeff doesn't remember much about the accident itself. But it was without doubt a pivotal event that brutally divided his life into a "before and after".

This is Jeff's story:

I went to the Gitanmaax reserve near Hazelton in search of a mask. A native mask to transform a dancer in a show I was working on. "That's all well and good," I was told, "but if you don't respect the noc-noc (the spirit of that mask), by telling the story, singing the songs, welcoming the mask to the community…the noc-noc will cause trouble." I was a skeptic. In my heart I didn't really believe all of this. None of us who are of European ancestry get it, nor will we ever.

A little while later I heard, "You want to be native, but you can't be, you're white." It dawned on me then that this wasn't really my business, that I was doing all of this for the wrong reasons. But I didn't care.

Then Sandford (the master carver) looked me in the eye and said, "I know why you're doing this, you're trying to reconcile cultures. But it's fake, it isn't true. There is one noc-noc whose existence is dedicated to reconciliation. I can make you a mask of that noc-noc, we'll pay tribute to it and to our desire to reconcile. You can use it for your reconciliation project and after the project we'll put it under glass until the next time it's needed."

When he told me this, all I could think was how absolutely perfect this was for my project, that it was just the right kind of authentic touch I needed for the show. I was so excited. But the carver followed up with an ominous warning, "Be careful of this noc-noc, it is a catalyst, it identifies what is wrong. If you're not being honest, it's going to let you know so that you can fix the dishonesty. The lesson of this noc-noc will be extreme. Make sure you're in this for the right reasons...."

Half an hour later, I was almost dead. I had been found guilty of cultural voyeurism, of being a con artist. The noc-noc saw right through me. I paid a price for my dishonesty, for messing with a power that was significant. The carver had warned me but I had not been honest. I had betrayed my instincts. The noc-noc looked straight into my soul and knew its truth. The noc-noc wanted me to learn.

My life until the accident was very much on track. I defined myself by my work, I was a self-admitted workaholic. I was birthing pieces that had life, a beauty, they were living beings.

After the accident, I became obsessed and inspired by the words of that Gitxsan carver and the noc-noc that saved me from dishonesty. It's paradoxical - I nearly died that day, in fact, a part of me did die, and yet I am convinced that the noc-noc saved my soul. My father was an Anglican minister and I have always been interested in the idea of G-d - its elusiveness, how to define G-d. I define myself and always have by my desire to search for some kind of truth, a kind of godliness, a sense of rapturous inspiration. My work was my compulsion to find that magic in service to others, to be the emotional vehicle for other people, to transport people to a special place. When I create – playing music, writing, composing, I am transported to a place where I am completely empowered. As a musician, an improviser, my talent is not my ability, it is my desire. Before the accident I was getting paid to create that place of beauty for other people. After the accident I became a lot more self-conscious. That is, more conscious of the mechanics of creating. I became distracted by the need to re-discover my past, to find my status again as a relevant composer. I had such a sense of loss, of disconnection. I just don't feel the same. It's strange - on the outside you look the same but inside you're completely different. You take your identity for granted. When your life is broken up, you lose connection to your past, to yourself. I could no longer connect things, everything became quite separated. I was able to write and play but it was all very technical, rigid, exact, like a Roman road. Technically it was all very good, but creatively, instinctively, I was lost.

My body, my brain - no longer had a sense of context, of social protocol and this affected my music. I was no longer able to integrate my ideas, information, things that inform other things. Everything became very compartmentalized. All my filters were gone. My decision-making was affected. I would get stuck before I even began with questions - how am I going to start this? How do I end? I could not choose anything, and I still can't. I was left with a compulsion, a drive to honour the idea, to tell the whole story in its entirety, not to leave anything out. I was drowning in a swamp of ideas, not being able to choose what was pertinent, relevant, and no longer able to articulate things the way I wanted.

I remember myself in flashes of images, how I was, but it's a character that is separate from me. To this day I am still trying to bridge the gap and truly connect with my past, to refined that confidence, the arrogance, the essence of who I was. When I look back at what I created before the accident I think - holy crickey - I was doing that? That's beautiful, how could I have been doing that? I don't have a connection to that person. This is the legacy. I'm continually in search of that place.

Candice James

The "Y" In Concussion You Don't See

Bonnie Nish

I have had two work related concussions. The first was in November of 2012, the next October 2013. This has nothing to do with my work other than they happened there. Fluke accidents in the workplace that left me disabled for over two years and to this day I still struggle and am not totally healed. Many people end up making headlines with concussions because they are huge hockey or football players. This is wonderful as it is bringing more attention to concussion syndrome and more understanding of the implications it has on a person's life. But what happens if you are just an ordinary person like me who has suffered a concussion?

Someone asked me the other day if I wonder why this happened to me. I answered honestly, that while that thought does cross my mind, it has been rare. For me this was just an accident. I happened to be in the wrong place at the wrong time. Yes, both times, but then I work in an elementary school where the likelihood of being hit by a basketball is far greater than if I worked in an office or even had been walking down the street.

Through the course of my concussion I have had many people ask the why and then try to provide me with the answers. Why did this happen to you? What do you think this meant? Before the concussion I had a very active life. Suddenly my entire life came to a standstill and I had to stop everything for over a year. The people around me couldn't help asking the why. They saw me struggle to get two words out. They saw that I couldn't drive, could barely walk, couldn't be in public, write or eat; they wondered what great plan this was for me and then why it happened. I understand this. For me, this why never became a part of the equation; however, I understand how it could for so many people going through this.

The why comes in other forms as well and these types of why's came into my life. They are also very important to address. On November 24th of 2012 just 22 days after I had been hit in the head originally, I ended up in the emergency department. Let me back up a minute here. I work in an elementary school as an Educational Assistant supporting children with disabilities. On November 2nd I was hit in the head by a child who was going across a zip line when he lost his balance. As I put my hand on his back to steady him, his head came whipping back and the back of his head got me right above my temple on the right side of my head. I immediately started to have symptoms even though I never passed out.

Over the next few days, the symptoms kept coming and I lost more and more of my abilities to do anything but sleep, cry and sleep some more. I was nauseous, dizzy, emotional, with headaches, losing words, stuttering and sensitive to bright lights, noise, smells and suddenly a wall came down and I couldn't eat. On Tuesday while trying to speak with a friend who was visiting I suddenly found I wasn't able to get words out. I could spell them, rhyme them, write them but I couldn't say them.

On November 15th, I had to defend my master's thesis even though I was already having trouble talking at times. I couldn't get certain words out. Luckily I could read out-loud fine. So, I read my thesis defense and I also had my computer to answer questions should I get stuck. My doctor who has been amazing throughout all of this gave me a note asking that I be allowed to do this should it be necessary. I didn't need to, luckily and I passed, no revisions. This was huge, considering my problems. However, for the next two days I couldn't move from my couch and I could barely speak. When I did speak it came out as sheer gibberish and my brother insisted I go to the emergency department, as he was afraid I might have had a stroke.

While the CT Scan was fine, they referred me to a neurologist. That being said, I spent 20 minutes with the neurologist. He didn't understand why I was having speech problems and doubted I had concussion syndrome. The neuropsychologist for the WCB head injury clinic I saw a few weeks later disagreed with him and thought my speech problems typical. The interesting thing though, was when he was testing me, suddenly I discovered, try as I might, I couldn't move my right hand to touch his finger when he held it up to his left side. His response. "Why can't you touch my finger?" Gee I don't know. I bit my tongue. I thought he was the expert after all and he should know the why. Apparently, not!

When I came home and tried to do this with family and friends I found the same thing. I had to literally force my right finger to try to touch theirs if they held it to the left of me. Why? I to this day don't know. My left leg was dragging when I walked and my left arm would sometimes go weak. I wasn't like this before the concussion. At a certain point I sat down to play the piano and was terrified when I realized I not only couldn't remember anything I knew but also couldn't play with my hands together.

About four or five months after the first head injury I was admitted to a WCB head injury clinic. The details of what went on there were both good and bad. From the get go, when filling out the assessment form to show how I was affected by the concussion, I was devastated. To see on paper everything that I was no longer able to do for myself was heartbreaking. The longer I was in the clinic, the more I realized I had lost so many of my abilities. Going out in the world made me have to get dressed everyday. Looking in my closet was overwhelming. I took to wearing the same three outfits, as trying to decide anything else was too much. I could never decide what to eat and I didn't really care if I ate. From the moment I was hit my taste buds and sense of smell became hyperactive. Because I couldn't drive or get on a bus without being sick, I took cabs back and forth. Depending on the driver this could also set off my symptoms. Sometimes I was ok, while with others, I wanted to throw-up as soon as I got out of the car and was dizzy.

Listening to some of the guys having a conversation about how impulsive they were made me realize I had become that way too. One of them said they could only keep $20 in their pocket. One day I got it in my head I needed a stationary bike at home. A friend who came by simply to drop off dinner ended up at my request, taking me to buy a bike. I didn't need it. I just couldn't get it out of my head. I found this about conversations. It didn't matter if I had told you something six times, once I started, even if I realized I had told you the story before, I had to finish it to the end. It didn't matter if I was stuttering I had to complete my thought. Although if I was stuttering, I usually forgot what I was trying to say by the time it stopped.

I met one other person in the clinic who also stuttered. He was hit on the same side of the head as I was. He had been assaulted and his symptoms were far worse than mine. When he finished his prescribed session at the clinic, he was sent back to work. He lasted one day and was back in to try to figure out why he wasn't able to cope at his job.

This brings me to one major issue that came up over the course of the entire time in the clinic and actually from the time I was hit. Everyone from the doctors to the OTs kept telling us how after 6 months most people totally recover from mild TBI. Suddenly it was the six-month mark and I wasn't back to my old jovial self, running poetry readings, hosting dinner parties, going out dancing or writing my PhD dissertation. I was barely able to stand being in public for a few hours at a time. and suddenly being even in small groups of people was causing me some anxiety. Why wasn't I getting better? People around me were either being sent back to work, whether they were ready or not, or abandoning the program. What was wrong with me that I couldn't make this benchmark that they were so adamant I should be making? I felt like such a failure! I wondered if I would ever get better. I wanted to know where their statistics came from. The response was, "Mainly young athletes." I kept reminding them, "I am not a 22-year-old bungee jumper, so how does this apply to me?" They insisted it did, showing me curves and graphs and statistics.

Over the last year and a bit I have had a number of people tell me I should be better in a certain amount of time. The first doctor I saw in a walk in clinic told me I should be better by Monday. This was Friday. Another told me I should be over it in three months. That was typical. Then at the clinic, I was told 6 months. I guess I am not typical and from those I have talked to, who have suffered concussions, they aren't either. Some still have symptoms to this day. Some took a year to four years to recover fully. I don't know the why of how long it takes for one person to recover fully and another not. There can be so many factors involved, I won't even hazard a guess as to why. There really is no room for the why in concussion, but it exists.

Why has it taken me so long to heal? I don't know. How do things look from this perspective? Well different. Some days seem very dark, some days are full of possibility and I can carve out new dreams. It depends on the day and how much I have done. I am still hopeful that I will regain more of my abilities, but if I don't, I am now prepared to shift, change, adapt. I can be different in this world. Sure the primary things are still the same, I love the green spaces, the ocean, the trees. But the time I have out in the world is significantly less. I am loving and craving the quietness of a forest or beach. I want to rest my brain because the best way to describe it when I do too much is that my brain just hurts, that if I put one more thing in there, it will literally explode.

It is very frustrating when you are used to doing things in a certain way and that way just isn't working anymore. It takes some time to accept this. My doctor explained it this way to me. She said, "A stroke patient who has lost the ability to use their arm must find new ways of dressing. The more they adapt, the easier it becomes to get dressed." It is the same for me. My brain just isn't functioning in the same way anymore, so I too must adapt and find new ways of being in the world. It is very much about who I am and how I relate in the world. Some days in the last two years I have felt angry about it. Some days I have felt without purpose. Other days I am just dammed determined I will find my way again. As my doctor said, it is all a part of the process of coming to terms and accepting.

So I come to the why in my concussion. Over the years people have asked me why it is I do all that I do. I do a lot. I run a charitable organization, Pandora's Collective, which I started in the literary arts. I work with children with disabilities in the school system and in the community. I have been a single mother raising my three children. I also write. I have started a private practice as an Expressive Arts Therapist and hope to get back to finishing my PhD. My answer was always because I can. Well now my answer as to why I have chosen to do this book is the same; because I can.

In the last two years so much of my life feels as though, at times, it has been robbed from me. Nevertheless, I am not one to sit idle for long and feel sorry for myself. I always find a way to change things. This book is something I can do. This is getting my life back. I am taking the bull by the horns. Maybe in sharing what it is like for me to be going through this it can help someone else. Maybe in bringing all these stories together it will make someone feel that there is some hope for them. I know in reading through these stories myself, I felt less alone, more connected and validated.

I can understand why some people feel so despondent after a concussion they start to think about killing themselves. At times I felt that way too. I wondered what my purpose in being here was when I could no longer do everything that I felt defined who I was as a person. I became despondent once, enough that I asked my doctor for a prescription for an anti-depressant and told her if I couldn't pull myself out of it in two weeks I would fill it. I pulled every trick I knew of out of my bag. I used painting, meditation, yoga, walking and writing when I could.

Slowly I began to see the fog that I was encased in lift. I leaned on my children and friends to remind me that I mattered to them no matter who I was. I found my why of existing again. If this helps one person to find a bit of hope through this mess or helps one person who is supporting someone going through this mess to understand a bit better, then it is worth putting myself out there. It is worth all of us sharing our stories.

I hope if nothing else you get something out of this and understand more deeply the why in Concussion. It may be different for you, non-existent for some and a plain pain in the butt for others. Wherever the why lies for you, know you are not alone. On that note I will stop as I have typed long enough. Now to figure out if I can find all my spelling mistakes before I sign off.

The Inner Workings of an Injured Brain Trying to Find the Way Home

Bonnie Nish

What I write here- so muted,
this impossible story I have carried for the last year,
a concussed brain weary
of a drumroll of irregular beats
marching down a road carved out by an accident.
My words become dead men, coming now six in a row,
walking timpanists who trip over one another
when the band master isn't looking,
the meter just a bit imbalanced.

I lie on my bed the slightest movement
causing the room to swirl
try to forget the indignity of losing self.
I lie still,
begin to visualize a big grey dog
on the front porch of a blue wood house,
I can feel the porch beams wrap tightly around him
and my narrative changes, even if briefly.
He watches herons rest,
the white oak across the street
sheltering the simple outcome of nesting
that eludes his gaze.
Then all at once everything begins to run from me
into a world that has its own story to tell.
The rocking chair behind him
stooped at an odd angle stopped,
arms dropped
an old man's breath lost mid-flight,
and the sudden explosion of a brain exploding.

On the other side of the road a baby,
a mother's full breast and lullabies
drapes a blanket across a chilling day.
The sound of a spirit shattering,
the herons disturbed search the sky
for unseen predators, and I remove myself
my head spinning with possibilities
of what is to come next.

Out-of-focus I turn to you-tube disaster videos
try to find my own sadness that hides
a blow to my body I can barely speak of.
My mind still hazy- bits of stories
that leak from a faucet I can't turn off,
the city where I met you lingers
pours out in an unrecognizable shape
no blissful reminiscence just something misplaced.
Herons wait for the sun to lift them
off a history wood pile now just a tiny blur
on a horizon that won't open.
A low-lying bridge over an ocean
threatening to collapse
and I can't cross over to glimpse a fuller picture.

I turn to my memory of you for help
realize too late you are only a hollow man
sitting on a dock fishing,
you could not hold the shade of night in the sky
or whisper in a dying soldier's ear
that their mother was waiting on the other side.
My stories slip behind a cloud
of metaphors I did not mean to use
to describe how empty I am left without you,
without identity, without my words.
Beyond the keys that bring letters into alignment-
engulfing fog.

Distant whimpers intrude
the constant buzzing between my ears,
the herons circle lower,
a dog caught in despair,
a new mother in just a night shirt
running across the street
to find an old man dead.
The moon swallows all of us
a blank book in my hands,
stories mixed together
stunned, hopeless, defiant,
to find the way home.

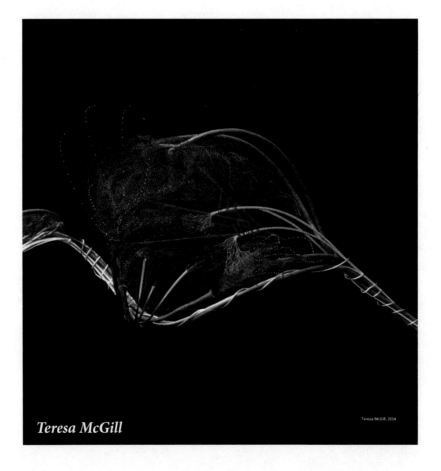

Teresa McGill

Teresa McGill, 2014

POSTSCRIPT 2016

Bonnie Nish

Just to let you know, even though this book has been a long time coming, I am doing more than ok. There have been gaps in the process simply because it was too hard to go back and revisit all of this. A whole year when I needed to walk away from the book and just live my life. My life has come back to me in chunks. I am back working in a high school full time. I am running Pandora's Collective Outreach Society's many events and then some. I am starting a new PhD program this fall in Language and Literacy Education at the University of British Columbia. I have started to work on a new manuscript of poetry. I am also planning a trip to Australia to see my daughter this year. I am back to yoga at least three times a week. I feel as though I have my life back.

Yet I am different. I still have to watch not to get too tired or I start to stutter. If I am not careful I feel overwhelmed and my brain just hurts as though it is a streetcar too full about to topple over. The buzzing in my head has never gone away but I have learnt to cope with it. However, most days I am thriving rather than just surviving. After all I have my words back and for a writer that is the greatest gift of all. I am grateful and will never take my thinking ability for granted again. It is a wonderful world and I am glad to be riding the subways, going out for dinner or to movies once more. I am back to all of the small and huge things that for over three years I couldn't do. I am just back!!

BIOS

Illustration 1 By Julie Reaper
Illustration 2 By Candice James
Illustration 3 By Teresa McGill

Editors

Bonnie Nish is founder and Executive Director of Pandora's Collective Outreach Society. She also sits on the editorial board of Room Literary Journal. Bonnie has been published worldwide in such places as The Ottawa Arts Review, The Danforth Review, Haunted Waters Press, Illness Crisis & Loss Journal Volume 24 and The Blue Print Review. Bonnie is a certified Expressive Arts Therapist who has worked extensively with at risk populations. She has a Masters in Arts Education from Simon Fraser University and is currently pursuing a PhD in Language and Literacy Education from the faculty of Education at The University of British Columbia. Bonnie's first book of poetry Love and Bones was published in the fall of 2013 by Karma Press. She is currently working on two new books of poetry.
www.pandorascollective.com   www.bonnienish.com

Nicole Nozick, raised in South Africa, earned a MA in Journalism and spent her early professional life in the Middle East working for the BBC, Reuters and the Associated Press among others. Now calling Vancouver, Canada home, Nicole is the Executive Director of the Vancouver Writers Fest where she is thrilled to combine her passion for writing and reading with her experience as a seasoned producer. Nicole was delighted to be part of this creative and thoughtful project.

Chelsea Comeau is a freelance writer and editor whose work has appeared in The Claremont Review, Quills, and CV2. In 2015, her chapbook What You Leave Behind was published by Leaf Press as the Canadian winner of the Overleaf Chapbook Contest.

Phyllis Bassett is a retired English teacher, social worker and lay chaplain. Two sons and a daughter call her variations on Mom and there are three young people whom she claims as grandchildren. She is working on a number of children's books, which she hopes to see published. She considers herself blessed to live in her heart's home, Vancouver. She feels living close to the ocean, the mountains and the giant trees is indeed one of life's great gifts.

Contributors

Ali Denno is an aspiring Poet and Screenwriter. Ali has been published on several online journals showcasing new writers. Her main focus is on mixing poetry and short film together. She graduated from Kwantlen Polytechnic University with a degree in Creative Writing and is currently working on her first manuscript of poetry.

Alastair Larwill lives and works in Ottawa, Canada. Once part of Messagio Galore sound poetry group, he now spends his time putting blankets around houses and throwing discs through holes.

Barbara Stahura, Certified Journal Facilitator, has provided guidance in harnessing the power of therapeutic journaling for healing and well-being since 2007, primarily for people with brain injury and family caregivers. She also presents programs on journaling for wellness that focus on gratitude and self-compassion, and other topics. Co-author of the acclaimed After Brain Injury: Telling Your Story, the first journaling book for people with brain injury, she also presents or has presented journaling events for state Brain Injury Associations/Alliances, the National Guard, people with cancer, equine-facilitated therapeutic groups, the National Association for Poetry Therapy, and others. A faculty member of the Therapeutic Writing Institute, she lives in Indiana with her husband, a survivor of brain injury. **http://www.barbarastahura.com**

Candice James is a poet, writer, visual artist, musician, singer-songwriter. She's in her 2nd three year term as Poet Laureate of New Westminster BC; Past President of both Royal City Literary Arts Society and Federation BC Writers; a member of LCP and TWUC and author of eight poetry books.

Dawn L. Metcalf, having written feature articles for Canada Wide Media, and Visual Imagination in Canada, the U.K. and U.S., as well as writing marketing collateral for business, theatre and other performance troupes, Dawn has a considerable list of nonfiction business, artistic and trade publication credits. Currently writing a collection of short stories taken from her life, when the call came to submit a story about head injuries, she knew she must write David's Story. Dawn is thrilled that the story is being published and hopes her words might resonate with other families who have experienced such trauma. When told that his story was being published David smiled and said, "Glad I could help!" I laughed and told him he had indeed.

Heather Williams was born, raised and educated on Vancouver Island. Dancing was in her soul and she studied it from a young age. She graduated from the Canadian College of Performing Arts then continued performed internationally. 7 ½ months into her contract at the inaugural opening of Universal Studios Japan 2001, she acquired a traumatic brain injury.

Now she is learning to redefine her new reality and purpose. She has written a memoir, 'Little Feet', which was cathartic and healing. She currently lives in Vancouver, British Columbia

Jeff Corness, since leaving SFU in 1986, has written over 80 compositions for dance, theatre, film and the concert stage, including 13 scores and 2 operas with Karen Jamieson Dance Company (with whom he served as composer in residence from 1988 to 1995). During this time, collaborations- including those with British company Foursight Theatre, and Phatravadi Theatre in Bangkok, Thailand -developed in him a passion for making interdisciplinary opera. In an attempt to address changes that have redefined his life since a near fatal car accident in 1995, Jeff is currently writing both the libretto and music for his fourth opera, called The BOOK of JONAH.

Jennifer Callaghan is retired and based in Toronto. Since receiving a major brain injury in a car crash, she has worked at building a new life, volunteering as a literacy tutor, editing a biography, and writing a book about her experience of brain injury and the long process of recovery.

Jude Neale is a Canadian poet with four poetry collections to her name. She is an award winning writer both nationally and internationally. She has joyfully collaborated with over fifteen other artists in the last two years - including creating a poetry manuscript called Line by Line with Bonnie Nish.

Julie Reaper was born July 26, 1958 in St. Agathe, Quebec. She spent her early years in Montreal, moved to Bermuda as a child, was educated in Switzerland, and graduated from Queen's University in Ontario with a degree in psychology. She was famous as "The Bird Lady" in Bermuda where she trained parrots for the Bermuda Parrot Theatre. Most recently, she worked as a care-giver. Julie passed away on December 20, 2015 at fifty-seven years old. Says Kim, "She was my best friend and partner for over 14 years, and I don't honestly know how I will live without her. She was like the sun sparkling on water; beyond beautiful..."

Karen Kristjanson, M.Sc. M.A., writes true stories to expand possibilities and reduce suffering. Her Beyond Limits Coaching practice is another way she supports people's growth. Karen's forthcoming book, *Harvest of Hope: Co-Parenting Stories* will be published in 2017. She is a contributor to the Huffington Post and DivorceMag.com. She lives in Surrey, B.C.

Kim Fink-Jensen is a mother of two precocious children and was working on her PhD when she was hit by a car. After leaving academia behind, she became a yoga teacher and moved to a small hobby farm to work as a nanny on the Sunshine Coast of British Columbia. She sometimes still needs to hide in a quiet room and remember to breathe.

Kim Seary, an award-winning actor, is also a poet, playwright, teacher, and story-teller. She is the founder and facilitator of Spirit Art, and also facilitates a weekly Centering Prayer meditation group. Kim is a companion for an elderly woman, a motivational speaker with MDABC Speakers' Bureau, and is currently studying peer support work and pottery making.

Kyle McKillop has collected four or five concussions, none of which came with cool stories. He teaches high school English in the suburbs of Vancouver, BC, and he's also a creative writing master's student. Connect with him online through kylemckillop.wordpress.com. Follow him on Facebook (facebook.com/kylemckillop) or Twitter (@kylemckillop)

Luanne Armstrong is an award winning multi-genre writer, editor and storyteller. She has published eighteen books of fiction, nonfiction, poetry and books for children. Luanne lives on her family's organic farm on Kootenay Lake where she lives with horses, dogs, cats and too many chickens.

Meg Stainsby is a writer and college administrator who lives in the Vancouver harbour on a floathome, amid seals, heron, eagles and crabs. She has recovered from her post-concussive syndrome and recently completed her third Master's degree—this one an MFA from the University in British Columbia.

Myna Wallin is a Toronto author and editor. She has had two books published: a collection of poetry, *A Thousand Profane Pieces* (Tightrope Books, 2006) and a novel, *Confessions of A Reluctant Cougar* (Tightrope Books, 2010). Myna received an Honourable Mention in the CV2 2-Day Best Poem Prize in

2009, and in 2010 she received an Honourable Mention in the Winston Collins/ Descant Prize for Best Canadian Poem. Last winter a poem of hers hung at the Art Gallery of Ontario, along with two paintings of Wallin, in an exhibit entitled, "Why (Not) Paintings of Poets?" Myna has her Master's Degree in English from the University of Toronto. ***www.mynawallin.com***

Susan Cormier, Métis multimedia poetry artist, has won or been shortlisted for such awards as CBC's National Literary Award, Arc Magazine's Poem of the Year, and the Federation of B.C. Writers' Literary Writes. Her current projects include Back Down the Rabbit Hole, an experimental documentary film about youth bullying.
Susan Cormier, wordworker
www.youtube.com/user/queenofcrows

Teresa McGill is a corporate training consultant and coach specializing in English communication and intercultural skills development. She holds a BA and TESL certification from the University of Toronto and studied Intercultural Relations at Pacific University. Teresa is a member of the Institute for Performance and Learning and TESL Canada.

Active in the language and communication training field since 1985, Teresa's areas of expertise include pronunciation training, presentation skills, business writing, leadership communication and intercultural dynamics. Teresa has designed and delivered business English skills training for hundreds of organizations in the corporate and public sector and she delivers Intercultural Dynamics training at University of Toronto's Rotman School of Management.

Teresa's innovative curricula and learning methodologies have been featured in articles in Human Resources and Management publications and in presentations at Canada's Language Industry Association, TESL Ontario, and the HR Summit. Her passion is helping internationally educated executives and professionals polish their English language skills, business communication strategies and intercultural fluency to enhance career success.